The Mosaic Map of Madaba
An Introductory Guide

The series Palaestina Antiqua was first published in Dutch by J.H. Kok Publishing House - Kampen. After consultation of the board it was decided to publish in English and German under Kok Pharos Publishing House.

1. H.J. Franken, Grondstoffen voor de materiële cultuur in Palestina en omliggende gebieden
2. J. Negenman, Een geografie van Palestina
3. C.H.J. de Geus, De Israëlitische stad
4. H.J. Franken, De puinhopen van het verleden
5. Antoon Schoors, Berseba - De opgraving van een bijbelse stad
6. R. van den Broek, J. Derksen, G. Mussies, K. Vriezen (red.), Kerk en kerken in Romeins-Byzantijns Palestina

New Series:

7. Herbert Donner, The Mosaic Map of Madaba
8. Ed Noort, Die Seevölker in Palästina

The Mosaic Map of Madaba

An Introductory Guide

Herbert Donner

Pharos

Kok Pharos Publishing House
Kampen - The Netherlands

CIP-GEGEVENS KONINKLIJKE BIBLIOTHEEK, DEN HAAG

Donner, Herbert

The mosaic map of Madaba: an introductory guide/Herbert Donner. -
Kampen: Kok Pharos. - (Palaestina antiqua, ISSN 0920-7422; 7)
Met lit. opg.
ISBN 90-390-0011-5
NUGI 644/633
Trefw.: bijbelse archeologie.

2nd print, 1995
Cover by Rob Lucas
Typesetting: Elgraphic bv, Schiedam
ISBN 90 390 0011 5
NUGI 644/633 W-boek

Preface

This booklet is not intended as an historical or even archaeological commentary on the mosaic map of Madaba. It is an introductory guide for visitors who want first and fundamental informations to help them understand what they see and admire. The guide need not be read straight through from start to finish, since numbers on the sketches included in the guide refer the user to the appropriate information in the booklet. A selected bibliography at the end provides further information.

A separate fold-out table has been included with this guide. On the front it contains a color reproduction of the mosaic map of Madaba. This is based on a drawing published by the architect P. Palmer and Prof. Dr. H. Guthe in ten lithographs in 1906. Of course, a drawing is not a totally exact reproduction of the original. It is presented here since there is no usable color photograph of the map as a whole and since the drawing is in itself a work of art which deserves to be heeded and used beside partial photographs (H. Donner and H. Cüppers, *Die Mosaikkarte von Madeba. Tafelband*. Abhandlungen des Deutschen Palästinavereins, Wiesbaden, 1977). The guide points out those places where the drawing differs too greatly from the original. The back of the fold-out table contains a sketch, made by Bart Oost, containing the numbers of the representations and inscriptions explained in the text.

This introductory guide is in many respects indebted to the studies which preceeded it, in particular some which are no longer in print such as the now slightly outdated work by M. Avi-Yonah, *The Madaba Mosaic Map*, Jerusalem, 1954. Avi-Yonah's commentary was occasionally used as a linguistic help in preparing the English manuscript.

I wish to express my indebtedness to Mr. Gary Martin and Mrs. C. Vanhove-Romanik who were kind enough to improve my English manuscript; as well as to offer thanks to Mrs. Dolly Füllgraf who prepared the final typescript.

The book is dedicated to the people of Madaba as a token of gratitude for their kind hospitality and help during the restoration work in 1965.

January, 1992 Herbert Donner

A Note for Arab Readers

Arab names are transcribed according to international linguistic conventions, as follows (clear equivalences not listed here):

'	=	ا
ṯ	=	ث
ǧ	=	ج
ḥ	=	ح
ḫ	=	خ
ḏ	=	ذ
z	=	ز
š	=	ش
ṣ	=	ص
ḍ	=	ض
ṭ	=	ط
ẓ	=	ظ
c	=	ع
ġ	=	غ
q	=	ق
y	=	ى

Contents

INTRODUCTION

In the early 1880's dissension arose among the Muslim and Christian inhabitants of *al-Karak* (coord. 217-066), east of the Dead Sea. Up to that time, the believers of both religions had lived peacefully together in the city. The problems soon led a group of Christians to leave their home town. After presenting a petition to the Turkish government in Istanbul, they were allowed to settle at Madaba (coord. 225-125), a vast artificial mound (Arabic *Tall*, mostly pronounced *Tell*) some 30 km south of Amman. The government gave permission to build churches, but exclusively on those spots where churches had existed in antiquity. There were, indeed, such spots - no wonder, since Madaba had been a flourishing city and a bishop's see during the Byzantine Empire, i.e. from the 4th to the 7th centuries A.D. Only in the Middle Ages did the city begin to decline, lose its wealth, fortune and importance, and lapse slowly - under Ottoman rule - into a poor, powerless village. Around 1850, Madaba was but a heap of rubble with few inhabitants, a wretched but venerable ruin.

The immigrants from *al-Karak* removed the debris from the still partially visible foundation walls of the ancient churches. During this work the Greek-Orthodox Christians discovered, in 1884, a marvellous mosaic map. It had been part of the floor of a large cathedral, but had become totally covered with debris and rubble. The surviving fragments of the mosaic were roughly repaired and incorporated in the floor of the new but smaller St. George's church.

His Beatitude Nicodemos, the Greek-Orthodox Patriarch of Jerusalem and All Palestine, was informed of the discovery that same year. But nothing happened; no one reacted to the news. More than a decade later, in 1896, when the librarian of the Patriarchate in Jerusalem, Reverend Father Kleopas Koikylides, came to Madaba, he saw the astonishing fragments of the mosaic map - about 30 square-metres - and immediately recognized its extraordinary value. He made an accurate and reliable preliminary sketch-map on graph paper and published a small commentary in Greek (1897), entitled: 'The Geographical Madaba Mosaic Map on Syria, Palestine and Egypt'. Subsequently, pilgrims started to visit Madaba, which was then out of the way and not easily accessible. These were learned, scholarly pilgrims rather than pious pilgrims. The numerous drawings, descriptions, articles and commentaries published by scholars from all over the world aroused international attention. In 1906 the first coloured reproduction of the Madaba map was published. The work, consisting of 10 lithographic plates based on drawings, not photographs, was edited by the architect P.

Palmer and by Professor Dr. H. Guthe, who were commissioned by the *Deutsche Verein zur Erforschung Palästinas* (German Palestine Exploration Society). It was an extraordinary creation, but not a faithful reproduction, since it was impossible to draw precisely the mosaic's 700,000 to 800,000 stones. In 1965 the German Society once more influenced the fate of the mosaic map. Generously subsidized by the *Stiftung Volkswagenwerk*, the map was thoroughly restored, preserved and protected by the present director of the Rhinian Museum at Trier, Dr. Heinz Cüppers, and by the museum's late restorator, Mr. Heinrich Brandt, under the direction of the present author. On November 15, 1965, the mosaic map was ceremoniously unveiled in presence of His Beatitude Benedictos I, the late Patriarch of Jerusalem and All Palestine, and numerous political and ecclesiastical dignitaries. In 1977 the first volume of the planned full study of the mosaic was published, written by H. Cüppers and by myself, containing photographic plates and a bibliography. The second volume, a detailed commentary and an introduction to Byzantine topography of Palestine and Lower Egypt, as far as it is represented on the map, will follow. The reader will find an introductory selected bibliography at the end of this guide-book.

I. Date and Fate of the Mosaic Map

The mosaic map of Madaba is one of our main sources for the character and topography of Byzantine Palestine both west and east of the Jordan river and the Dead Sea, as well as of Lower Egypt. It is the oldest existing map of Palestine apart from a small section of the so-called Peutinger Plates (*Tabulae Peutingerianae*). These plates, now in Vienna, constitute a road map of the whole Roman-Byzantine Empire which was used mainly for administrative purposes. Although originating in the 4th century A.D., this 'road map' is preserved only in a medieval copy. The Madaba map was created in the 6th century, most probably during the reign of the emperor Justinian (527-565). The basis for this dating of the map is to be found in its general style and, more important, its special contents.

Matters of style are difficult to determine. Mosaic pavements on church floors were quite common in the Christian Byzantine Empire round about the Mediterranean Sea. A general stylistic comparison with other examples does not lead to persuasive conclusions. The chances for dating the mosaic map by concentrating on the comparative interest in similar themes and representations are not much better. Certainly, there are comparable mosaic representations of cities or villages: e.g., from Antioch around 450 A.D. (D. Levi, *Antioch Mosaic Pavements I, 1947, p. 319*), from the churches of St. John Baptist and St. Peter and Paul at Jerash dated 529-533 (J.W. Crowfoot, *Churches at Jerash. British School of Archaeology in Jerusalem, Suppl. Papers 3, 1931, pl. VII and XII*), and - above all - the wonderful mosaics from *Mā^cīn* (coord. 219-120) dated 719/20, now restored by the Franciscan Fathers on Mt. Nebo (R. de Vaux, *RB 1938, pl. XII-XIII*), and recently those of the church of St. Stephen at *Umm ar-Raṣāṣ* (M. Piccirillo, *Chiese e mosaici di Madaba, Jerusalem 1989, p. 269-308*). All of them have a different style from that of the Madaba map. They give pictorial views of cities seen from the front. This manner of depiction can also be found on the Madaba map, but to a smaller degree. The larger and more important cities and villages are depicted in a manner similar to our city maps, seen from above, in a bird's eye view - and for this exact parallels do not exist. Nevertheless, from a stylistic point of view the representations on the Madaba map can be put between those of the Jerash and of the *Mā^cīn* and *Umm ar-Raṣāṣ* mosaics, nearer to the Jerash mosaics than to the others. The style does not contradict the proposed date.

These considerations, however, need to be supplemented by the contents. The mosaic map looks like a cartographic illustration of two pilgrims' reports from the 6th century: the first one written by the archdeacon Theodosius (between 518 and 530), the other one by an anonymous pilgrim from Piacenza (shortly after 570). We may add the so-called *Breviarius de Hierosolyma* (Short Description of Jerusalem) from about 550 containing only a description of the Holy City. Naturally, not everything that these reports describe can be found on the Madaba map. The purposes are different, and sometimes the mosaic artist suffered from lack of space. Therefore, we should not make the mistake of using arguments from silence to reach a more exact date for the map. Some observations, however, are indeed useful for that goal. In the representation of Jerusalem we notice the New Basilica of the Mother of God, the so-called *Nea Theotokos* (see section D, nr. 12), built by emperor Justinian and consecrated on November 20, 542. It is clear, the mosaic must be later than this date. Furthermore, four churches represented on the map are first mentioned by the Anonymous of Piacenza: the churches of Galgala (nr. 26), of the Egyptian Martyrs near Ascalon (nr. 92), of St. Victor near Gaza (nr. 120), and of Zacharias (nr. 84). If we take into consideration that Palestine was devastated in 614 by the Persians under Chosroes II, we can draw the following conclusion: the Madaba map was created in the second half of the 6th century A.D., perhaps even during the lifetime of Justinian, i.e. before 565. There are no arguments to support a more exact date.

Unfortunately, it is difficult to reconstruct the history of the church and its map. The mosaic shows traces of several sorts of damage and repair. At some unknown point in its history the church was consumed in flames. Joists and girders crashed upon the precious mosaic and damaged parts of it, especially the region representing Neapolis (see nr. 32 and p. 45) where the mosaic stones were charred. Other parts may have been completely destroyed by this catastrophe, e.g. a large section in the center (Dead Sea) and parts beyond the present edges. Did the Persians cause this catastrophe in 614? We do not know. Still other damages were repaired in antiquity by re-using cubes of the pavement itself, notably representations of living beings, such as the sailors on the Dead Sea or the lion pursuing a gazelle in the eastern Jordan Valley, as well as some inscriptions. This fact points to iconoclasm, either by the famous iconoclast Yazid II (720-724) or by bedouins at later times. It seems possible that St. George's church at Madaba was still used in the 8th century, since Madaba surrendered to the Muslims and was not conquered and destroyed. In this case, its destruction by fire would have happened later. During the Middle Ages the Madaba churches were unused. Later, the remains of the mosaic map were eroded again and again, for example by tomb-diggers, causing the foot-shaped damages in the Dead Sea, by the climate, by rodents such as voles, and finally by the reconstruction of the church after 1884. At that time, when the pillars were erected and set into the mosaic, repairs were made by using plain cement, mostly greyish or brownish.

II. Character and Geographical Value of the Map

The surviving remains of the mosaic map are most impressive and instructive. The Holy Land with Jerusalem in its center – the 'navel of the earth' – is seen from the west. It is represented in such a way that the viewer could fancy himself standing on a high position in the west or hovering above the Mediterranean Sea. The map is oriented to the east, not to the north, corresponding to the orientation of nearly all Christian churches. The preserved fragments show the Jordan river running into the Dead Sea, the eastern mountains up to *al-Karak* (Charachmoba, nr. 11), the northern part of the central Palestinian mountains up to *Nāblus* (Neapolis, nr. 32), the southern part of the same mountains up to *al-Ḫalīl* (Hebron, nr. 82) and *Bēt Ğibrīn* (Eleutheropolis, nr. 87), the hill country west of the mountains, the Palestinian coastal area with *Asdūd* (Ashdod, nr. 89 and 90), *ᶜAsqalān* (Ashkelon, nr. 91) and *Ġazza* (Gaza, nr. 118), the southern desert with *Bīr as-Sabaᶜ* (Beersheba, nr. 99), parts of the Mediterranean and, finally, the Nile Delta. The present extent measures about 10.5 m in length and about 5 m in width. If we take into consideration the nonuniformity of the fragments, the surface area of the extant fragments is approximately 30 square-metres. For this 700,000 to 800,000 mosaic cubes were needed.

The present extent, however, is not the original one. To the north (that is, to the viewer's left) there are two isolated fragments belonging to the map (see below p. 97f.): A. a part of Galilee; B. a part of the tribal area of Zebulun. A third fragment (C.) showing Sarepta (*Ṣarafand*), now totally obliterated, may not have been part of our map. Fragment B is situated about 10 m left of Jerusalem. We may suppose that the map extended roughly to the southern part of the Phoenician coast. To the south it is self-evident that Mount Sinai, Alexandria and the monastery of St. Menas, Memphis and Heliopolis were represented, perhaps even Thebes. To the east the original map ended just beyond *al-Karak* (Charachmoba, nr. 11), where the desert begins. A screen separated the mosaic map at this point from the so-called *schola cantorum*. Most probably, Damascus, Bostra (*Boṣra eski Šām*) and Philadelphia (Amman) were also depicted, and remains of an inscription referring to Petra are preserved (nr. 16). To the west, the Mediterranean Sea is the natural border. There is reason to presume the representation of some ships; traces of one of them are still visible (see nr. 66), those of another were visible after 1884 (Fragment B, see p. 97-98). According to the archaeological investigations made during the restoration work in 1965, the original map measured about 15.60 m in length and 6.00 m in width = 93 square-metres.

The details represented refer to the physical and historial geography of Palestine and Lower Egypt. In the main, we have to distinguish three kinds of representations:

1. The background, especially deserts, plains and larger valleys in yellowish white, mountains in brown, green, blue, pink and yellow, waters in blue, brown and black.

2. The symbols of cities, villages, churches, other buildings, human beings, animals, plants, natural features of different kinds etc. We need not go into too much detail here; a few remarks will suffice. We see, for example, in the eastern Jordan Valley the hind legs, the tail and traces of the head of a lion pursuing a gazelle looking anxiously backwards, fishes in the Jordan river and in the arms of the Nile, and even traces of a nice little crocodile at the upper edge of the Nile. The most common plant is the date-palm, many of which are shown, but there are also thorn bushes on both sides of the Jordan river, a terebinth near Mambre (nr. 82), and indefinable plants beneath Betomarsea (nr. 12). Two ships are sailing on the Dead Sea, each of them with a crew of two and heaps of salt or barley. A smaller unmanned ship is found on the Sebennitic arm of the Nile. There are likely traces of a ship in the Mediterranean beneath the sanctuary of St. Jonah (see nr. 66). The mosaicist used several modes of reproduction for cities and villages. For larger cities – such as Jerusalem, Neapolis, Lydda/Diospolis, Jamnia, Eleutheropolis, Azotos Paralos, Ashkelon, Gaza, Charachmoba, Pelusium – he preferred a kind of oblique pictorial representation. These cities are seen from a western elevation (like the whole map), showing both city-walls and buildings inside the city. The western wall is seen from outside, the eastern from inside. Where necessary the buildings are turned upside down to show more façades than could be seen in real perspective. These pictorial representations depend on the Hellenistic-Roman tradition for depicting cities as demonstrated other mosaics. The distinguishing feature, however, is exactness. What we have here appears to be an early form of a city-map. For medium-sized cities – such as Jericho, Orda, Elusa etc. – the artist used symbols resembling those of Hellenistic-Roman origin, i.e. these cities are seen from the front, having 1-3 gates and 4-5 towers in their walls, the gable roofs of the buildings rising up above the walls between the towers. Larger villages are shown in a more conventional

manner: with 3-4 towers, 1-2 gates, sometimes without gable roofs. Small villages have the simplest shape: 2 towers and 1 gate. In addition to cities and villages, the map depicts single buildings and constructions. These are mainly churches of basilical type - always with red roofs and yellow triangular pediments -, but also cisterns and founts, bathing-establishments (Kallirrhoë, nr. 10), memorial buildings (the sanctuaries of Saints), two Jordan ferries, a watchtower near Jordan river etc. - on the whole, an astonishing variety and richness of representations.

3. The Greek inscriptions. These are found in various styles: black on a bright background, white on a dark background, red for texts of special importance. Some belong to cities or villages, others recall Biblical events or quote Biblical texts. The script is the revived oval script with ligatures and some abbreviations ($\overline{\Theta C}$ for ΘEOC God, $\overline{KC}$ for KYPIOC Lord etc.). The inscriptions will be explained later in this guide-book.

What is the geographical value of the Madaba map? First of all, we have to state the following basic judgement: the Madaba map is not a collection of nice little pictures with inscriptions in order to illustrate the Holy Bible. It is a real geographical and topographical map. It is cartographically correct to a considerable degree and is not only the oldest but also the most exact map of Palestine before modern cartography which dates no earlier than the nineteenth century. The cartographical accuracy can be recognized in both physical and historical details. Look, for example, at the mountains east of the Dead Sea: they show the characteristic dislocation of the mountain range, forming three mountain levels. Other examples are the flow of the Jordan river in sinuous curves, like a meandering stream, or the change of direction of the *Wādī Zarqā Mā*^{c}*īn* (see p. 36). The positions of deserts, plains, valleys and mountains are as correct as the general shape of the Dead Sea or of the Nile Delta. Even if the artist suffered from lack of space, he sought for the utmost exact representation of topographical details, for example, in the plain of *Nāblus* which extends from west to east, but is turned up to the south on the mosaic map, the symbols being in correct relationship to each other. The reader will find more details in the extensive description of the map.

Naturally, there are some larger or smaller geographical and topographical inaccuracies, but they cannot diminish the high value of the map. Some of these errors are easily and clearly explicable. To give some examples:

1. The eastern shore of the Dead Sea is too large, and strangely enough there is no indication of the peninsula *al-Lisān* which is visible from all quarters. Especially in the area of *Wādī Zarqā Mā^{c}īn* (see p. 36) the representation seems to be wrong. The *Wādī* does not flow through a wide shore, but comes directly out of the mountains going through a relatively deep canyon into the Dead Sea. This strangeness, however, can be explained. If we assume that the mosaicist was a native of Madaba or at least lived there, it is probable that he knew the region from his own view, also the hot springs of Baaras (*Ḥammām Zarqā Mā^{c}īn*). If this be so, he used the old road from *Mā^{c}īn* downwards which is still used today. On the way, the mouth of the *Wādī* is visible more than once from above: as a wavy plain carved by the gorge of the *Wādī*, very similar to what is shown on the map.

2. The artist was not very familiar with the area south of the Dead Sea, for he made the *Wādī'l-Ḥasā* run directly into the Sea, whereas it comes out of the mountains and enters first the *Ġōr aṣ-Ṣāfī*.

3. Other interesting inaccuracies are related to the Mediterranean coast. This sea-shore also is too large, the distance between Ashdod and its harbour (nrs. 89 and 90) is too great. Above all, however, the coast-line between Palestine and Egypt is obviously wrong. In reality, the coast-line of the Mediterranean turns west south of Gaza, but on the mosaic map it turns east. In this case, the reasons are altogether clear. To draw the coast-line correctly, the mosaicist would have had to abandon the rectangular size of his map: the coast-line now going from top to bottom, and the Nile with its arms coming from the right side – entirely impossible on a church floor! Moreover, a conflict would have been produced between real geography and religious geography, since in ancient Christian tradition the Nile was one of the rivers of Paradise, and the Paradise was situated in the east, according to Gen. 2:10-14. Therefore, the Nile had to run from the east to the west without any regard to the geographical truth, even though people may have well known it. In fact, on the Madaba map the Nile does run from east to west, parallel to the rivers Arnon and Zered.

4. Another problem was produced by the size of some representations. The mosaicist wanted to depict Jerusalem much larger than any other city or village, because Jerusalem was the most important city of all and the 'navel of the earth'. Furthermore, he needed a large space for the benedictions on the tribes of Joseph and Benjamin (nrs. 28 and 41). Thus considerable displacements were caused in the central mountain area and

in the Judaean hill country. Cities and villages were shifted either to the south, as were Bethoron (nr. 55) and Nikopolis (nr. 73), or to the east, as Bethel (nr. 45) and Gibeon (nr. 50). Consequently, villages in the vicinity of the ones just mentioned were displaced as well. The mosaicist was compelled to such displacements by lack of space. Some irregularities in the geographical latitude may be due to the same cause.

5. Occasionally the mosaicist followed erroneous traditions as to the location of Biblical places. He did so in the cases of Ajjalon (nr. 47), Jethor (nr. 103), Madebena (nr. 116) and others.

To repeat: observations such as these do not alter the fact that the mosaicist created a marvellous, unique and extraordinary map of Palestine and Lower Egypt, a map which is much more reliable than it seems to be at first glance.

Up to this point we referred to the 'mosaicist' or the 'mosaic artist'. It is impossible to identify the anonymous artist more precisely. Some scholars have advocated the hypothesis that a certain Salmanios could have been the author of the map. This Salmanios worked on the approximately contemporaneous mosaics of the church of the Apostles at Madaba, but that is all we know of him (P. Thomsen, *ZDPV 52, 1929, p. 169f.*). As to our map, inscriptions reveal neither the donor nor the artist or artists. At any rate, we may imagine the presbyters of the congregation as commissioners of the mosaic, but this is a mere assumption. Finally, we do not know who suggested decorating the church floor with a map: a map as some kind of illustration of God's salvation history according to the Holy Bible. There is reason to believe it was a learned priest or rather a bishop or a monk. We should continue to speak of the 'mosaicist' or 'mosaic artist', as of some sort of 'corporate personality' consisting of the inventor and intellectual father as well as the chief of the artists and artisans who worked on the spot.

III. Sources of the Map

The Madaba mosaic map is full of detailed information on the topography and history of Byzantine Palestine. It is undoubtedly clear that the mosaicist did not invent these data. He needed and used literary sources available in a library at Madaba. Fortunately, we are able to specify some of the sources from which he took his information – and this, in turn, gives insight into the level of education and the condition of the library at Madaba in the second half of the 6th century.

The question of literary sources for the Madaba map cannot be answered easily and should not be answered hastily. Interpreters need critical ability in no small degree. For not every item in literature which is in harmony with the details represented on the mosaic map ought to be considered a source of the map. In other words, we have to be cautious in reconstructing the library of Madaba! We shall try to describe the problems and to distinguish as precisely as possible matters of fact from mere suggestions.

1. Beyond any doubt, the primary and general source of the Madaba map was the Holy Bible in Greek, the so-called Septuagint. To avoid misunderstandings: the Bible is not so much the source of the details as it is of the general idea. God's salvation history with mankind is a Biblical idea, and therefore the Bible is the main prerequisite for its cartographical representation, from the patriarchs (see the oak of Mambre, nr. 82) to Jesus Christ's death and resurrection (see the church of Holy Sepulchre in Jerusalem, section D, nr. 7). Some details are derived directly from the Bible – it is peculiar – almost exclusively from the Old Testament. We find

a) the territories of some ancient Israelite tribes, allotted to them by casting lots according to Josh. 13-19, and therefore called 'The lot of XY': Ephraim (nr. 39), Benjamin (nr. 42), Dan (nr. 64), Judah (nr. 78), and Simeon (nr. 107).

b) three texts from the blessings of Jacob (Gen. 49) and of Moses (Deut. 33), and from the song of Deborah (Judg. 5): 'Joseph, God blessed you with the blessing of the earth that possesses everything, and again: blessed of the Lord be his land' (nr. 28), 'Benjamin, God shields him and dwells in between his mountains' (nr. 41), 'Dan, why does he remain in ships?' (nr. 65).

c) five inscriptions referring to certain events mentioned in the Bible: 'the wilderness where the serpent of brass saved the Israelites' (nr. 21), 'the wilderness of Sin where the manna and the quails were sent down' (nr. 97), 'Raphidim where Israel fought against the approaching Amalek' (nr. 98), 'Rama, a voice was heard in Rama' (nr. 76), and the only example from the New Testament '(the sanctuary) of St. Philipp where Candace the eunuch is said to have been baptized' (nr. 81 with an explanation of the mosaicist's error!).

2. Apart from the Holy Bible the mosaicist knew and used the oldest geographical lexicon to the Bible: the famous *Onomasticon of Biblical Place Names*, written in Greek by the bishop Eusebius of Caesarea around 320 A.D. and translated into Latin by St. Jerome shortly before 400 A.D. (abbreviated *Eus.On.*). This invaluable lexicon was not only the main literary source for the Madaba mosaic map, but is still one of the main sources for us in our topographical research of Byzantine Palestine. The mosaicist used it exhaustively: 61 of altogether 149 inscriptions of the present fragmentary map are derived directly or indirectly from Eusebius' Onomasticon. We have to distinguish between several kinds of reference: real quotations, excerpts, renderings with or without corrections. Above all, the mosaicist used the Onomasticon whenever he tried to locate places by transposing information into the map sketch. He followed Eusebius, repeated his errors or corrected them implicitly. This can be demonstrated by the following examples:

a) The village of Thimnah where Judah, Jacob's son, went from Adullam to shear his sheep – according to Gen. 38:12f. – is described on the map as follows: 'Thamna where Judah sheared his sheep' (nr. 71). This inscription is literally taken from Eusebius' Onomasticon 96:24-26: 'Thamna where Judah sheared his sheep. There is still a large village in the area of Diospolis half-way going up to Aelia (= Jerusalem). It belongs to the tribe of Dan or Judah.' The mosaicist also followed Eusebius' localisation. Although Thimnah = *Tall Baṭāšī* 8 km south of *Abū Šūša*, seems to be wrongly located on the map north of Nikopolis (*ᶜAmwās*), this is deceptive: for whereas Thimnah is located correctly, Nikopolis, by reason of lack of space, is too far to the south.

b) The native place of the prophet Micah is described as 'Morasthi whence was Micah the prophet', and a nearby church '(the sanctuary) of St. Micah' (nr. 86). The text is borrowed from *Eus.On.* 134:10f. Eusebius calls the village 'Morathei', but St. Jerome transcribed it 'Morasthi'. The location is 'east of Eleutheropolis' (= *Bēt Ǧibrīn*). If we take into consideration that Eusebius used no more than the four main directions north, east, south, and west (there is no such thing as north-east etc.), the village – *Ḫirbat Umm al-Baṣal* near *Tall al-Ǧudēda* – is correctly located on the map. The church of St. Micah, however, is missing in the Onomasticon. It was built later and is first mentioned in St. Jerome's description of the pilgrimage of St. Paula and Eustochium, ch. 14 (around 400 A.D.).

c) The Biblical village of Zoar (= *Tall Tall Šēḫ ᶜĪsā* near *aṣ-Ṣāfī*) is described as 'Balak, also Segor, now Zoora' (nr. 18). The inscription is derived almost literally from *Eus.On.* 42:1: 'Bala, which is Sigor, now Zoora', and is located correctly. The place name Balak differs from Eusebius' Bala, but is identical with the form given by the Septuagint in Gen. 14:2; and here we also find the more common orthographical form Segor instead of Sigor. In this case the mosaicist seems to have corrected Eusebius with the aid of the Greek Bible.

d) The inscription belonging to Biblical Gerar (= *Tall aš-Šarīᶜa* or *Tall Abū Ḥurēra*) runs as follows: 'Gerara, royal city of the Philistines and border of the Canaanites to the south, where the *saltus Gerariticus* (= the domain of Gerar) is' (nr. 102). In *Eus.On.* 60:7-14 we read: '**Gerara** from which the **Geraritike** is named, situated beyond the Daromas, 20 miles south of Eleutheropolis. It was the ancient **border of the Canaanites to the south**, and a **royal city of the Philistines**. It is situated, according to the Scripture, "between Kadesh and Shur", two deserts: one of them adjoins Egypt, and the people reached it after crossing the Sea of Reeds, the other one, Kadesh, extends to the desert of the Saracens.' The mosaicist obviously made a excerpt from Eusebius' text (the words in fat type), supplementing it by the administrative term *saltus Gerariticus* which is often mentioned in Byzantine literature.

e) The village of Sychar (= *al-ᶜAskar* northeast of *Nāblus*) is briefly described as 'Sychar, now Sychora' (nr 34). *Eus.On.* 164:1-4 gives more detailed information: 'Sychar, before Neapolis, near the portion of land which Jacob gave to his son Joseph. According to the Gospel of John, Christ spoke there to the Samaritan woman at the well. It exists till to-day.' It is noteworthy here that Eusebius located the Lord's talks with the Samaritan woman (John 4) in Sychar itself, while the mosaicist listed Jacob's well separately and at its traditional place, near modern *Balāṭa* and opposite Joseph's tomb.

f) Looking for Biblical Ajjalon 'where the sun stood still' (Josh. 10:12f.), we find on the Madaba map: 'Ailamon where stood the moon in the time of Joshua, son of Nun, one day' (nr. 47). The text of *Eus.On.* 18:13-16 also mentioning the moon instead of the sun, runs differently: 'Ailom, a valley where the moon stood when Joshua prayed, near a village that is still called Ailon, three miles east of Bethel. Nearby are Gabaa and Ramaa, the cities of Saul.' Eusebius apparently followed an erroneous tradition, for Ajjalon was not situated east of Bethel, but near Nikopolis (*ᶜAmwās*) in the hill country west of *al-Ǧīb*: it is identical with *Yālō*, a village now totally destroyed. This correct location was well known already in antiquity, as we may learn from St. Jerome, for example, who added to his translation of Eusebius' passage the following (19:16f.): 'but the Hebrews affirm Aialon to be a village near Nikopolis, at the second milestone on the way to Jerusalem.' This is quite correct, but the mosaicist did not take note of it. Probably, St. Jerome's translation was not at his disposal, in any case he complied with Eusebius' false location.

g) The last example deals with two famous mountains in the vicinity of *Nāblus*: Gerizim (*Ǧabal aṭ-Ṭōr*) and Ebal (*Ǧabal Islāmīya*). These mountains are represented twice on the Madaba map (nr. 33): near Jericho and near Neapolis. What has happened here? The problem can be solved on the basis of *Eus.On.* 64:9-17 where, strangely enough, both mountains are indeed located near Jericho. Eusebius, however, does not fail to add: 'The Samaritans show other ones near Neapolis, but they are wrong, for the mountains shown by them are too far from each other, so that it is impossible to hear one's voice when calling to each other.' Although this seems to be entirely intelligible and is confirmed by Deut. 27, the Samaritans were by no means wrong. Eusebius was wrong, and everybody knew it, perhaps he himself included. The Samaritans laid claim to the mountains, considering them to be their own holy mountains. Hostility to the Samaritans forced the orthodox Jews in Jerusalem to locate both mountains at another spot, for the Samaritans were not allowed to be right. Eusebius followed the orthodox Jewish tradition. The mosaicist, however, being well informed, preferred a Solomonic solution: he listed the mountains twice, indicating by larger letters that he regarded the location near *Nāblus* as being correct.

3. It is difficult to point out other literary sources of the Madaba mosaic map. Undoubtedly they did exist. The abundance of details on the map is best explained by the assumption of a well-stocked library in Madaba. Unfortunately, there is no evidence to substantiate this assumption definitely. It is not enough to state the identity of a place name on the map with a place name in a literary source. Further information and check points are needed. It is, for instance, highly probable that the

Madaba library possessed at least two works of the famous historian Flavius Josephus, the *Jewish War* and the *Jewish Antiquities*. These works were written in Greek and were held in great esteem. Did the mosaicist use them several times, as suggested by some scholars? We cannot exlude it, though we have nothing but the identity or similarity of some place names here and there, and that is not sufficient. Furthermore, we may suppose that works of the Early Fathers were at hand in an ecclesiastical library, especially the Bible commentaries by Origenes and St. Jerome. But is it really true, and did the author of the map use such books? We do not know. Finally, it is much more difficult to establish sources for places which are attested only in later literary works, such as John Moschus' *Pratum Spirituale* ('the Spiritual Meadow'), the commentary on Gen. 10 called 'the Distribution of the Earth', or in Latin or Greek pilgrims' reports. All suggestions of that kind remain doubtful.

4. Certainly, the mosaic artist used Byzantine road-maps. As for us, we only know a single map of that sort: the so-called Peutinger Plates (*Tabulae Peutingerianae*), originating from the 4th century and preserved in a medieval copy. These plates contain a road-map of the whole Byzantine Empire. But there were, of course, regional maps as well, for the purposes of civil and military administration, for the Byzantine mail etc. On the Madaba map only one road is really represented in white cubes: the first section of the junction road between Jerusalem and Neapolis, starting from the Damascus Gate (*Bāb al-ᶜAmūd*). Other roads are not represented, it is true, but indicated by mile-stations and sites along the road:

a) The road from Jerusalem to Bethoron, Lydda/Diospolis and to the Mediterranean coast is indicated by two mile-stations: 'the fourth milestone' (nr. 53) and 'the ninth milestone' (nr. 54). Moreover, the following main cities or villages are represented along this road: Bethoron (nr. 55), Nikopolis (nr. 73) and Diospolis (nr. 61). It is interesting to see that Nikopolis is located too far to the south, by reason of space restriction rather than because the mosaicist was not familiar with the site.

b) The Jericho-Skythopolis road is indicated by some places having no Biblical reference, being merely road-stations: Archelais (nr. 23), Phasaelis (nr. 22), Koreus (nr. 4) and Salumias (nr. 3). Of course, Skythopolis (*Bēsān*) was represented on the map, but is unfortunately broken.

c) The Jerusalem-Hebron road cannot be identified positively, because all sites along it are of outstanding Biblical importance, and are shown on the map on this basis: Bethlehem (nr. 77), Bethzur (nr. 80), the sanctuary of St. Philipp (nr. 81) and Hebron itself (nr. 82). The same is true of the road between Jerusalem and Eleutheropolis (nr. 87) and of other roads as well.

d) Completely clear, however, is the indication of the most important coastal road connecting Palestine with Egypt. The mosaicist listed nearly all cities, villages and stations along this road from Gaza (nr. 118) to Pelusium (nr. 134): Thauatha (nr. 114), Raphia (nr. 122), Betylion (nr. 123), 'the border between Egypt and Palestine' (nr. 124), Rhinokorura (nr. 125), Ostrakine (nr. 126), Kasin (nr. 127), Pentaschoinon (nr. 128) and Aphthaion (nr. 129). All these names are well known from Byzantine and later sources.

5. Most probably, there were Byzantine itineraries in the Madaba library. We know this genre of literature from the famous collection called *Itinerarium Antonini*. The mosaicist seems to have used such itineraries, mainly when preparing the representation of the Nile Delta. For details see the description and explanation (p. 79-86). Did he use itineraries and Byzantine city-lists as sources for other sections of this map? Possibly, but we can not say for sure. We find places, e.g. in the southern desert, which are not mentioned in the Bible or in Eusebius' *Onomasticon*, but are well known from the works of Georgios Cyprios, the church history of Sozomenos, from the so-called *Notitia Dignitatum* (an administration handbook) and from itineraries: Mampsis (nr. 93), Elusa (nr. 104), Photis (nr. 105), Orda (nr. 106), and others. The same might be true for the Roman-Byzantine fortifications in the *Wādī 'l-^{c}Arabā*: Prasidin (nr. 94), Thamara (nr. 95) and Moa (nr. 96) – perhaps even for Aia (nr. 13) and Tharais (nr. 14) east of the Dead Sea.

6. Finally, we have to pay attention to the mosaicist's own familiarity with the land, or at least with certain of its parts. Without such an intimacy he could not have delineated the sections of the map so correctly. Look, for example at the area east of the rift valley: the threefold dislocation of the mountain range, the characteristic run of the *Wādī Zarqā Mā^{c}īn*, the buildings at Kallirrhoë (nr. 10), and the situation of Charachmoba (nr. 11) on the top of a mountain. For all these and more details the mosaicist's intimate knowledge was the first prerequisite. The same is true for certain sections on the west bank, e.g. for the area southwest of Jerusalem, and even for the plain of *Nāblus* the sites of

which are represented topographically correct, although the plain itself is turned to the south due to lack of space. As to Lower Egypt alone, it is doubtful whether the mosaicist ever saw this land. The reader will find considerations concerning this problem below (see p. 79-86).

IV. Technique of the Mosaic

If we take the probable total surface area of 93 square-metres as a basis, as mentioned above (p. 17), we can make the following calculation. The number of mosaic stones used in one square-decimetre is at most 150 in the most elaborate sections. Let us take an average of 120 cubes: in this case the total number of cubes would be about 1,116,000. An expert mosaic artist is able to place about 200 cubes per hour. Consequently, a workman would need a total of approximately 5580 working hours, or 558 working days of ten hours each. That is, a team of, let us say three workmen directed by a superior artist would have needed about 186 days. The time for preparations, such as laying of the foundation, cutting of the cubes etc. must be added.

The workmen used mosaic stones of very different colours, all of them being available in the land east of the rift valley: white, black, at least four shades of red, several shades of green-blue, dark brown, violet, pink, grey, yellow, yellowish-white etc. They also used cubes of glass: in a sort of golden-yellow for triangular church pediments, for the dome above the Holy Sepulchre in Jerusalem, for windows and gates; in a high green for the fresh water in the river Zared (*Wādī 'l-Ḥasā*); in dark green for the crocodile in the Nile. On closer inspection, the cubes are spikes, up to 2 cm square and about 6 cm long, many of them broken during the long and eventful history of the mosaic. Smaller spikes were used for the representations of larger cities, men, animals, and plants. The foundation beneath the mosaic was made threefold as follows (from bottom to top): an earthen floor of 7-10 cm, a plaster-floor of 15-20 cm made of lime mortar and pulverized charcoal in which limestones up to the size of a fist are embedded, finally the actual bed made of a relatively solid lime slip being somewhat leafy at the bottom side.

Some conclusions on the method of laying the mosaic may be drawn from the mosaic map itself. At first, the superior mosaic artist made a drawing either by scratches or by outlines of coal or ruddle, thus delineating the map. Then, the major geographical features were laid out, beginning with chiefly black boundary lines, such as mountainous areas, the Dead Sea with the Jordan river, the Mediterranean with its coast-line, the arms of the Nile. Afterwards, the inscriptions and larger cities were fitted in, at last the smaller symbols for villages. In the plains, however, the mode of action was reversed: at first the symbols for cities and villages, and then the inscriptions fitted into the spaces in between. Occasionally, there are symptoms of what is called *horror vacui* (aversion to leave vacant places): the mosaicist filled the empty spaces not only with animals, plants, ships etc. but also with symbols having no inscription. In most instances those symbols are stop-gaps, only here and there the workmen could have forgotten to lay out the inscriptions.

Of course, in the ancient church no pillars or columns were set into the mosaic, as happened in the new one. The mosaic map lay like a transept in front of the *schola cantorum* and the altar, visible from all sides. The builders of the new church in the last century took pains to preserve the fragments of the map. Dr. Heinz Cüppers wrote in his preliminary report on the restoration work (*ZDPV 83, 1967, p. 15*) as follows, translated from German: 'In spite of laying new foundations of the exterior walls and in spite of erecting the massive stone-pillars, both producing some smaller damages, we may affirm that the builders of the present church and the discoverers of the mosaic put much care into preserving the parts of the map exposed, much more care than was usually given at that time. The erosion of the map occured long before, when the ground was used as a cemetery, and the builders of the new church must not be accused.'

V. Sense and Purpose of the Map

Finally, we need to inquire into the purpose or the purposes of the Madaba mosaic map in order to determine its sense and to estimate its value for the investigation of Palestinian history and topography in Byzantine times. We search for the reasons why the inventors or commissioners did not rest content with an ornamental or figurative mosaic to be laid on their church floor but preferred a mosaic map of the Bible lands. Whose idea was this? For what reason and by whom was it realized? We may fancy that it was the bishop of Madaba who had the idea, or perhaps a learned clergyman - that is obvious. But who was actually able to realize it? It is difficult to think of one of those firms who offered mosaics to the Christian or even to the Jewish communities by sending agents with sample-bags: most probably, they had no map of Palestine and of the surrounding countries in their collection. There must have been a very clever and most qualified mosaic artist in Madaba itself or from elsewhere who was able to understand the intentions and wishes of the inventor and to translate them into a mosaic work. No one should say: money answers all things. Artists of such caliber are not offered for sale. On the other hand, however, money was obviously no object at Madaba. For a mosaic of such kind was of course much more expensive than the usual mosaics we find on church floors.

We may distinguish between inferior and superior purposes of the mosaic map. To begin with, one of the inferior purposes was the intention to offer information for Christian pilgrims, to show them how they were to go from one holy place to another. We have to think of pilgrims not from everywhere but from the countries east of the rift valley, probably in the main from Madaba itself and from its surroundings. The occidental pilgrims whose reports are preserved, seldom or scarcely visited those countries, and if they had done so, the map would have been of little avail for them. One of the superior purposes, however, is the realization of the exceptional idea, totally unknown before the 6th century, to illustrate God's salvation history in a map. On the mosaic map both Testaments, Old and New, are represented and the holy sites are displayed to the spectator's eyes. Further purposes can be considered, for example a clear liturgical function. The holy liturgy realized and actualized God's salvation history, and the map visualized it. Jerusalem in the center of the map - and of the world -, and the Holy Sepulchre built by the emperor

Constantine as the center of Jerusalem underline this idea. Moreover, the members of the congregation could come into direct contact with the holy and promised land: they could tread upon it, of course not with shoes but barefoot - as Moses did according to Exod. 3:5: 'Take off your sandals, for the place where you are standing is holy ground!' The numerous symbols of churches and memorial buildings inside and outside the cities and villages - conspicuously not of monasteries! - also refer to church history as a continuation of God's salvation history. And, last but not least, we note an educational purpose of the map: the church of God introduced herself not only as an institution for the salvation and redemption of mankind but also as a teacher and master of Christian culture.

Let us admire the cartographical achievement of the mosaic artist! Using different literary sources and supplementing them by his own familiarity with the holy land he created a unique object: the oldest known map of Palestine and Egypt, a map more reliable than all its successors up to the beginning of modern cartography in the 19th century.

DESCRIPTION AND EXPLANATION

To facilitate the synopsis, the Madaba mosaic map is divided here into four sections, from the left to the right (i.e. from north to south), each being described and explained separately. First, the physical features of the map will be described, then the symbols and inscriptions according to their numbers on the map sketch. Explanations of the inscriptions are organized as follows: first the inscription itself (line 1: in Greek capital letters as on the map; line 2: in Greek minuscules; line 3: transliteration and translation into English), followed by references (from the Bible, from Eusebius' *Onomasticon*, and from other literary sources), finally comments on identity and other interesting factual matters. Letters in brackets are restored. Points underneath letters indicate that the letters are not completely preserved. The inscriptions are written without any spaces between the words. In this commentary, however, spaces are left in order to make it easier to read the texts.

I. Section A

The Jordan river meanders in the Jordan Valley and runs into the Dead Sea. East of the Dead Sea and its shore, being somewhat too large, we see the threefold dislocation of the mountain range towards the rift valley. We note the following tributaries of the Jordan river and the Dead Sea from the east: the mouth of river Jabbok (*Nahr az-Zarqā*) near the northern ferry, scarcely visible on the spot of an ancient repair; *Wādī Zarqā Mā*^c^*īn* with its characteristic change of direction from north – south to east – west; river Arnon (*Wādī'l-Mūǧib*); river Zared (*Wādī'l-Ḥasā*) wrongly represented as if running directly into the Dead Sea. Three fish swim in the Jordan river; remains of a fourth can be seen on the left. The fish on the right side is well advised to swim against the stream, by that he is kept alive. East of the Jordan river, a lion whose destroyed body has been scantily repaired, is pursuing a graceful little gazelle. Gazelles exist in Palestine even now, though less than in former times. Lions, well attested in the Bible and in other literary sources, have retired to inner Africa; the last ones were mentioned in the Lives of Saints and Monks from the Middle Ages, e.g. in the *Pratum Spirituale* by John Moschus. Here and there we see palm trees in the Jordan Valley and on the sea shore, indicating the presence of fresh water, mostly near villages, thorn-bushes or the so-called apple of Sodom (*Calotropis procera*). The Jordan river is crossed by two ferries passing along ropes across the river. It is difficult to determine their exact places, because the Jordan river often changed its bed and flow in the soft marly soil. We may, however, start from the assumption that the ferries were at the most employed crosswalks between the east and the west bank. If this is true, the northern one might have been in the area of present *Ǧisr ad-Dāmya* (coord. 200-167, although it is represented north of the mouth of river Jabbok which could have changed its bed as well), and the southern one at modern King Hussein Bridge (coord. 201-142). Near the southern ferry we see a watch-tower built upon an arch with a ladder leading up to it, probably constructed so because of the floods. This watch-tower was used by a military garrison to protect and control the crosswalk. Military posts of that kind are attested in the so-called *Notitia dignitatum* (74: 47f.): *cohors prima salutaria inter Aeliam et Hierichunta* 'the first cohort *salutaria* between Jerusalem and Jericho' (= *Ḫān Haṭrūr*, coord. 184-136) and *cohors secunda Cretensis iuxta Iordanem fluuium* 'the second Cretian cohort near the Jordan river' (= our watch-tower).

The Dead Sea, strangely enough without any indication of the peninsula *al-Lisān*, shows blue-greyish waves and seems to be lashed about by wind blowing from north to south as is clear from the two ships on the Dead Sea. The left one is being rowed, with its sail folded. It has a crew of two, almost completely destroyed and roughly repaired: the left one is rowing, and the right one seems to be the commander. This ship is carrying some sort of whitish material - perhaps salt -, and is heading north. The other on the right with two standing sailors is moving southward with an open sail. The yellowish stuff might be wheat. There was, indeed, trading navigation on the Dead Sea in antiquity. Remains of harbours have been found near *al-Mazra*ᶜ (coord. 201-077) in the northern part of *al-Lisān*, and at the northern end of the Dead Sea. The commercial products were salt, perhaps potash, and wheat from the highland of Moab which was transported through *Wādī 'l-Karak* down to the Dead Sea.

On the mosaicist's mistakes in representing the eastern shore of the Dead Sea, especially in the area of *Wādī Zarqā Māᶜīn* and *Wādī 'l-Ḥasā*, see above p. 19 and 36.

① [ΑΜΜ]Α̣Θ̣Ο̣Υ̣Ϲ̣

'Αμμαθοῦς

Ammathus

A place of problematic identity; perhaps *Tall al-Ḥamma* (coord. 197-197) south-west of *Bēsān*? (H. Donner, *ZDPV 83, 1967, p. 21*). No traces of this inscription can be seen on the drawing.

② ΑΙΝѠΝ Η ΕΓΓΥϹ ΤΟΥ ϹΑΛΗΜ

Αἰνὼν ἡ ἐγγὺς τοῦ Σαλημ

Ainon near Salem

The text is quoted from the Gospel of John 3:23 and *Eus.On.* 40:1-4. Ainon (from Semitic *ᶜayn* 'spring') is one of the traditional places where St. John the Baptist was said to have baptized; it is also mentioned by the pilgrim Etheria, ch. 15:1-6. It was situated in the vicinity of Salumias (nr. 3). The bluish-green cubes above the inscription seem to indicate the garden with its spring and pool as described by the nun Etheria.

③ ϹΑ̣[ΛΟΥΜΙΑϹ]

Σαλουμιας

Salumias

Eus.On. 152:4ff. (not in the Greek text, only cited by Procopius of Gaza and translated by St. Jerome), also mentioned as Sedima in Etheria, ch. 13:3-14:3. The village is probably identical with *Ḫirbat Ḫisās ad-Dēr* near

Tall ar-Ridġā (coord. 199-200), about 12 km south of *Bēsān*. It was one of the traditional places where the king and priest Melchizedek was said to have met Abraham according to Gen. 14:18-20 (H. Donner, *ZDPV 83, 1967, p. 20f.*).

④ ΚΟΡΕΟΥC

Κορεους

Koreus

Josephus, *Jewish War* I:6:5 (§ 134); the place may also be mentioned on the Peutinger Plates (Coabis?). Koreus was one of the road stations on the road from Jericho to Skythopolis (*Bēsān*). It is identical with *Tall al-Mazār* (coord. 195-171) in the lower *Wādī 'l-Fār^ca*, situated in an area called *Qarāwa* which has kept the ancient name. The landmark of Alexandreion (*Qarn Ṣarṭaba*) is nearby.

⑤ ΑΙΝΩΝ ЄΝΘΑ ΝΥΝ Ο CΑΠCΑΦΑC

Αἰνὼν ἔνθα νῦν ὁ Σαπσαφας

Ainon where now is Sapsaphas

This Ainon (see nr. 2) is another place where St. John the Baptist was said to have baptized. It was situated in the *Wādī 'l-Ḫarrār*, opposite the present baptism place, on the east bank of river Jordan (H. Donner, *ZDPV 81, 1965, p. 26-28.55*). It is mentioned by some Christian pilgrims and monks (e.g. Pilgrim of Piacenza 9; Epiphanius Monachus Hagiopolita IX:18-X:2; John Moschus, *Pratum Spirituale* [PG 87,2851]). The name Sapsaphas is derived from the Semitic word for willow (arab. *ṣafṣāf*). The symbol underneath shows an enclosed spring and something shaped like a conch. Neither the church nor the monastery, both built by the patriarch Elias of Jerusalem († 518) and mentioned by John Moschus, are represented on the map.

⑥ ΒЄΘΑΒΑΡΑ ΤΟ ΤȢ ΑΓΙȢ ΙΩΑΝΝΟΥ ΤȢ ΒΑΠΤΙCΜΑΤΟC

Βεθαβαρα τὸ τοῦ ἁγίου 'Ιωάννου τοῦ βαπτίσματος

Bethabara, (the sanctuary) of St. John of the Baptism

Gospel of John 1:28 (the name Bethania used there has been corrected by a remarkable number of manuscripts into Bethabara) and *Eus.On.* 58:18-20. The site is also mentioned by nearly all Christian pilgrims and Early Fathers. It is identical with *Dēr Mār Yuḥannā*, the present place of Holy Baptism, near *^cAyn al-Ġaraba*. The church represented on the map was built by the emperor Anastasius (491-518); see the archdeacon Theodosius, ch. 20.

Northeast of the Dead Sea, in the southern Jordan Valley, two medium-sized cities are represented, the northern one fragmentarily, the southern one almost completely preserved. The inscriptions belonging to them are lost. The identity of these cities, however, is undisputably clear, for there were only two cities in this area.

⑦ [(ΒΗΘΝΑΜΡΑΝ Η ΚΑΙ) ΒΗΘΝΑΜΒΡΙϹ]

(Βηθναμραν ἡ καὶ) Βηθναμβρις

(Bethnamran, also) Bethnambris

Numb. 32:3.36; Josh. 13:27; *Eus.On.* 44:16-18. The site is identical with *Tall Nimrīn* (coord. 209-145) near the mouth of *Wādī Šu*^{c}*ēb* (H. Donner, *ZDPV 83, 1967, p. 22f.*). The Hellenistic-Roman-Byzantine city succeeded the older one on *Tall al-Blēbil*, called Beth-Nimra in the Old Testament.

⑧ [ΒΗΘΑΡΑΜ (or ΒΗΘΡΑΜΦΘΑ) Η ΝΥΝ ΛΙΒΙΑϹ (or ΙΟΥΛΙΑϹ)]

Βηθαραμ (or Βηθραμφθα) ἡ νῦν Λιβιας (or 'Ιουλιας)

Betharam (or Bethramphtha), now Livias (or Julias)

Numb. 32:36; Josh. 13:27; *Eus.On.* 48:13-15. The Old Testament town was called Beth-Haram, later on, under the Roman emperor Augustus, it was called Livias or Julias. It is identical with *Tall Iktanū* and the small but remarkable *Tall ar-Rāma* (H. Donner, *ZDPV 83, 1967, p. 22f.*).

It appears to be situated at the upper course of *Wādī Zarqā Mā*^{c}*īn* which runs into the Dead Sea after its turn (see p. 36)

⑨ [ΘΕΡΜΑ Β]ΑΑΡΟΥ

Θερμὰ Βααρου

The hot springs of Baaras

Fl. Josephus, *Jewish War* VII:6.3 (§§ 178-189); *Eus.On.* 44:21-46:2; Petrus the Iberian (Raabe 87-90). These famous thermal springs, continuously used since antiquity, are identical with modern *Ḥammāmāt az-Zarqā*, situated in the gorge (lower course) of *Wādī Zarqā Mā*^{c}*īn*, reachable from Madaba and *Mā*^{c}*īn* on a road whose traces can probably be seen left of *Wādī Zarqā Mā*^{c}*īn*, between the palm-tree and the *Wādī* (H. Donner, *ZDPV 98, 1982, p. 175-180*).

⑩| ΘΕΡΜΑ ΚΑΛΛΙΡΟΗϹ

Θερμὰ Καλλιρόης

The hot springs of Kallirrhoë (i.e. beautiful spring)

Fl. Josephus, *Jewish War* I:33:5 (§§ 656-658) and *Antiquities* XVII:16:5 (§ 169); Plinius, *nat. hist.* V:16; also mentioned by many Christian,

Jewish and Arab authors. The hot springs of Kallirrhoë, situated at *ᶜAyn az-Zāra* on the eastern shore of the Dead Sea, became famous because King Herod the Great (37-4 B.C.) stayed there before his death at Jericho and his entombment at Herodeion near Bethlehem (*Ǧabal Furēdīs* or *Fardēs*). The mosaicist represented three of the constructions there (from left to right): a round pool from which water flows into the Dead Sea; a square reservoir with an apse (a so-called Nymphaion), also with a water course to the sea; a building bisected by a wall or dam to which water flows from the foot of the mountains and from which water runs into the sea, probably a bathing reservoir with flowing hot water which could be mixed, when required, with cooler water or minerals. Remains of these constructions can be seen there even now, although they are difficult to interpret (H. Donner, *ZDPV 79, 1963, p. 59-89*). The bathing reservoir mentioned in the third place might be identical with what people call *al-Madaš*. Two palm-trees indicate the abundance of water and the fecundity of this area.

(11) [ΧΑΡ]Α̣ΧΜΩΒ[Α]

Χαραχμωβα

Charachmoba

This is modern *al-Karak* (coord. 217-066), situated on the top of a high mountain, seen from the west. Its name, sometimes mentioned by Greek and Latin authors, is composed of χάραγξ 'palisade' and Moab, the country east of the Dead Sea: fortress of Moab. Unfortunately, we do not know anything about Byzantine *al-Karak*; the mosaic map is our only source. The representation shows the mosaicist's attempt to depict the main buildings of the city he knew. The city is shown as a walled fortress. In the south, we see a gate flanked by two towers, and nearby, east of it, a church with a red roof. Two colonnaded streets run from south to north, the central one leading to a big church, probably the cathedral. Charachmoba is known as a bishop's see. In front of the cathedral we notice a circular object, partly damaged: brownish cubes in the center, black and white cubes around. This cannot be the gate of the church (compare with the door of the southern church!), it is rather a sort of circus surrounded by a street. – Above the inscription, i.e. east of the city, there are remains of a simple representation of a village which cannot be identified.

(12) ΒΗΤΟΜΑΡϹЄΑ Η Κ̷ ΜΑΪΟΥΜΑϹ

Βητομαρσεα ἡ κ(αὶ) Μαιουμας

Betomarsea, also Maiumas

The representation shows a somewhat obscure building: a central dome flanked by two vaulted side-wings or a theatre with annexes. Beneath the building there are unidentifiable plants and perhaps flowing water, apparently indicating the exceptionally luxuriant vegetation and water on the spot. The most probable identification is with *ᶜAyn Sāra* at the foot of the hill of *al-Karak* (H. Donner, *ZDPV 98, 1982, p. 181-183*), now a recreation center with restaurant, park and swimming pool. The spring itself provides the necessary water for modern *al-Karak*. Betomarsea was the house of a cultic congregation or club, and Maiumas the name of a popular licentious feast with water amusements and symposia, widespread in the ancient Near East, but in the vicinity of *al-Karak* only attested on the Madaba map.

(13) ΑΪΑ

Αια

Aia

The village, mentioned nowhere in Byzantine sources, is identical with *Ḫirbat ᶜAy* (coord. 211-060) in the *Wādī'l-Fuḫēt*, about 6 km southwest of *al-Karak* (H. Donner, *ZDPV 98, 1982, p. 183-188*).

(14) ΘΑΡΑΪϹ

Θαραις

Tharais

This village, not mentioned in Byzantine sources, is identical with *al-ᶜIrāq* (coord. 211-055) near *ᶜAyn Tarᶜīn* in the *Sēl Ǧudēra*, 5 km south of *Ḫirbat ᶜAy* (nr. 13).

(15) [Ζ]ΑΡΕΔ

Ζαρεδ

Zared

Num. 21:12; Deut. 2:13f.; *Eus.On.* 92:10. This is the ancient Biblical name of *Wādī'l-Ḥasā*.

(16)

At the edge of the mosaic, south of river Zared (nr. 15) and on the right of the inscription Zared, two and a half black letters are visible (only on the original map, not on the drawing): ΜΕΛ̣|Α̣|Δ̣| (not depicted on the sketch). The following restoration is suggested (H. Donner, *ZDPV 98, 1982, p. 188-191*):

[ΠΕΤΡΑ ΕΝ ΓΗ ΕΔΩΜ ΤΗϹ ΑΡΑΒΙΑϹ Η Κϛ ΙΕΧΘΟΗΛ Η Κϛ ΡΕΚΕΜ ΕΝΘΑ ΕΠΑΤΑΞΕΝ ΑΜΕϹϹΙΑϹ ΤΟΝ ΕΔΩΜ ΕΝ ΓΗ]ΜΕΛ̣[Α]

Πέτρα ἐν γῇ 'Εδὼμ τῆς 'Αραβίας ἡ κ(αὶ) Ιεχθοηλ ἡ κ(αὶ) Ρεκεμ ἔνθα ἐπάταξεν Αμεσσιας τὸν 'Εδὼμ ἐν Γημελᾷ

Petra in the country of Edom, province of Arabia, also Joktheel, also Rekem, where slew Amaziah Edom in Gemela.

The text is restored and combined from *Eus.On.* 142:7-8; 144:7-9; 110:22; 72:28-29. It refers to II Kings 14:7 (where the 'Valley of Salt' is misinterpreted in the Greek Septuagint version as if it were a place name Gemela). If this restoration is principally accepted, other slightly differing wordings are conceivable. If it is not accepted, other proposals are most welcome.

(17) [ΑΛ]ΥΚΗ Η ΚΑΙ ΑCΦΑΛΤΙΤΙC ΛΙΜΝΗ Ḥ [ΚΑΙ ΝЄΚ]Ṛ̣Α ΘΑΛΑCCΑ

'Αλυκὴ ἡ καὶ 'Ασφαλτῖτις λίμνη ἡ καὶ Νεκρὰ Θάλασσα

Salt, also Pitch Lake, also the Dead Sea

The inscription is almost literally derived from *Eus.On.* 100:4-5.

(18) ΒΑΛΑΚ Η Κ/ C[ΗΓΩΡ Η ΝΥΝ] ΖΟΟΡΑ

Βαλακ ἡ κ(αὶ) Σηγωρ ἡ νῦν Ζοορα

Balak (= Bela), also Segor (= Zoar), now Zoora

Gen. 14:2; 19:22f.; *Eus.On.* 42:1-5; 94:2; 150:20; also mentioned by other Greek, Latin, Hebrew and Arab authors. The site is identical with *Tall Šēḫ ᶜĪsā* (coord. 195-048) near *aṣ-Ṣāfī* in the *Ġōr aṣ-Ṣāfī*, southeast of the Dead Sea. In Byzantine times the city was an administrative center and a bishop's see. The symbol is that of a medium-sized town with two red-roofed churches.

(19) ΤΟ ΤȢ ΑΓΙȢ Λ[ΩΤ]

Τὸ τοῦ ἁγίου Λωτ

(The sanctuary) of St. Lot

This church, conventionally represented, is attested only on the Madaba map. It was a memorial church of Abraham's nephew Lot (= *an-Nabī Lūṭ* of the Holy Qur'an) who spent a night together with his two daughters in a cave not far from Zoar (nr. 18) according to Gen. 19:30-38, and became the father of Ammon and Moab. The site was discovered in 1983 by H. Donner and E.A. Knauf. It contains ruins of a chapel and two caves above the right bank of *Wādī 'l-Ḥasā*, near its egress from the mountains, near *aṣ-Ṣāfī* (not yet published).

(20) ЄΡΗΜỊ[Α]

'Ερημία

The desert

This is the northern part of *Wādī 'l-ᶜArabā*.

(21) ЄΡΗΜ̣[ΟϹ ЄΝΘΑ/ΟΠΟΥ] ΤΟΥϹ ΙϹΡΑΗΛΙ̣Τ̣Α̣Ϲ̣ Є̣Ω̣Ω̣Ι̣Ν (?) Ο ΧΑΛΚ̣Ο̣ΥϹ ΟΦΙϹ̣

Ἐρῆμος ἔνθα/ὅπου τοὺς Ἰσραηλίτας ἔσωσεν (?) ὁ χαλκοὺς ὄφις

The wilderness where the serpent of brass saved (?) the Israelites

This text refers to Numb. 21:6-9: the story according to which Moses put up a bronze snake on a pole in order to save the people bitten by venomous snakes. The strange sequence of letters marked by a question mark seems to be a mere error in writing.

II. Section B

This section shows the following geographical features: the westernmost part of the southern Jordan Valley, the western part and the shore of the Dead Sea, the central Palestinian mountains from Neapolis (*Nāblus*) to Hebron (*al-Ḫalīl*), the coastal plain, and two fragments of the Mediterranean Sea. The representation of Jerusalem is not included here (see section D).

We see in this section three tributaries of the Jordan river and the Dead Sea: brooks coming from the west, from the so-called desert of Judah. We may wonder whether they are representations of real brooks, or mere indications of the fact that numerous brooks descend from the mountains to the rift valley. Considering the remarkable geographical accuracy in other parts of the map we prefer the first assumption. If this is correct the northernmost brook may be identical with the *Wādī an-Nār* (Kidron Valley), beginning in Jerusalem, although not running into the Jordan river but into the Dead Sea. The only imposing *Wādī* running directly into the Jordan river in this area is *Wādī 'l-Qilṭ*, but its mouth is in the latitude of Jericho. The southernmost brook in the latitude of Hebron and Mamre is most probably identical with *Wādī ᶜArēğa*, flowing into the Dead Sea near *ᶜAyn Ğidī*. The middle brook might belong to the system of *Wādī at-Taᶜāmira* (*Wādī Mšāš* or *Wādī al-Ġuwēr*?). It is represented too far to the south when seen from the Dead Sea shore, but correctly when seen from the villages upon the mountains - Thekoa and Bethlehem - which are displaced to the south because of the space devoted to Jerusalem.

The central Palestinian mountains are represented similarly to those east of the Dead Sea, with multicoloured cubes and swinging lines. The mountainous area is sometimes interrupted by plains of white or yellowish cubes, as follows: 1. the plain of *Nāblus*/Shechem, turned from west-east to north-south because of lack of space (see above p. 18); 2. the plateau following the watershed line on the top of the mountains, visible near Jerusalem, Bethlehem, up to Hebron; 3. two plains near Theraspis and Nikopolis probably belonging to the hill country west of the mountains.

There are four damaged pieces of the mosaic in this section. First of all, a large one in the center of the whole map, repaired in the last century and again in 1965 in plain cement. Also badly damaged is the northernmost part of the section: the area around Neapolis (*Nāblus*). Here the mosaic was burned in a catastrophe we cannot date. Unfortunately, its details are hardly visible. Finally, two damaged pieces in the south: east of Mamre and east of Ashdod; both of them had been repaired in antiquity by reusing cubes from the map itself. We may assume that some living beings were shown on these spots, at least a small animal or some such in the vicinity of *ᶜAyn Ğidī*.

The representation of Ashkelon (nr. 91) is shown on a separate fragment between the harbour of Ashdod (nr. 90) and Gaza (nr. 118).

(22) [ΦΑCΑΗ]ΛΙC

Φασαηλις

Phasaelis

Fl. Josephus, *Jewish War* I:21:9 (§ 418), also mentioned by some Early Fathers and other Byzantine sources. Phasaelis was one of the road stations on the road from Jericho to Skythopolis (*Bēsān*), built by Herod the Great and named after his brother Phasael. It is identical with *Ḫirbat Faṣāyil* (coord. 191-159).

(23) ΑΡΧЄΛΑΪC

Αρχελαις

Archelais

Fl. Josephus, *Antiquities* XVII:13:1 (§ 340); XVIII:2:2 (§ 31); also mentioned on the Peutinger Plates. Archelais was one of the road stations on the road from Jericho to Skythopolis (*Bēsān*), built by Archelaus, son of Herod the Great. It is identical with *Ḫirbat al-ᶜŌğa at-taḥta* (coord. 194-195).

(24) ΤΟ ΤȢ ΑΓΙȢ ЄΛΙCΑΙΟΥ

Τὸ τοῦ ἁγίου 'Ελισαίου

(The sanctuary) of St. Elisha

Fl. Josephus, *Jewish War* IV:8:3 (§§ 459f.); Procopius of Gaza, *de aedificiis* V:9; also mentioned by many ancient Jewish, Christian and Muslim authors. It is the memorial church of the prophet Elisha (II Kings 2:19-22) above *ᶜAyn as-Sulṭān*, the spring of prehellenistic Jericho, situated at the foot of *Tall as-Sulṭān* (coord. 192-142). We see a red dome-shaped roof between two towers, and a wall with one gate. The spring was protected by the wall, and the red roofed memorial building was erected above the spring. A water-course runs from below the right tower to Jericho – the Byzantine Jericho (nr. 25) –, supplying the city's oasis.

(25) ΊΕΡΙΧΩ

Ιεριχω

Jericho

Josh. 2; 6; also mentioned by most ancient Jewish, Christian and Muslim authors. Byzantine Jericho was situated south of its prehellenistic predecessor (*Tall as-Sulṭān*), beneath the present townlet *Arīḥā* (coord. 193-140). Nine palm-trees indicate the abundance of water and the fecundity of the oasis. The representation is that of a medium-sized town with a wall, four towers and two gates, with three churches inside, two of them with red roofs and one with a yellow triangular pediment. Unfortunately, we cannot identify these churches.

(26) ΓΑΛΓΑΛΑ ΤΟ ΚΑΙ ΔΩΔΕΚΑΛΙΘΟΝ

Γαλγαλα τὸ καὶ Δωδεκαλιθον

Galgala (= Gilgal), also the Twelve Stones

Josh. 3-4; *Eus.On.* 64:24-66:7; also mentioned by nearly all Christian pilgrims and many Early Fathers, the church first described by the Pilgrim of Piacenza, ch. 13, shortly after 570. This is the Byzantine sanctuary of Biblical Gilgal recalling the twelve stones the Israelites took up when crossing the Jordan river and carried to their first station beyond. It is still unidentified, but was undisputably situated near Jericho. The most recent proposal for Biblical Gilgal, not necessarily identical with the Byzantine one, is *Suwwānat aṯ-Ṯanīya*, about 2 km northeast of Jericho (B.M. Bennet, *PEQ 104, 1972, p. 111-122*). The Pilgrim of Piacenza describes the twelve stones as 'in the basilica behind the altar'; the mosaic artist, however, showed them outside the church to make them visible for viewers.

(27) ΑΛΩΝ ΑΤΑΘ Η ΝΥΝ ΒΗΘΑΓΛΑ

῞Αλων Αταθ ἡ νῦν Βηθαγλα

The threshing-floor of Atath (= Atad), now Bethagla (= Beth Hoglah)

The threshing-floor of Atad, situated beyond the Jordan river (i.e. on the east bank), where Joseph and his brothers mourned for their father Jacob (Gen. 50:10f.), and the Biblical place Beth Hoglah (Josh. 15:6; 18:19.21) which is identical with *Qaṣr Ḥağla* (coord. 197-136) near *ᶜAyn Ḥağla*, were first combined by *Eus.On.* 8:17-20.

We now turn to the central Palestinian mountains, to the region that is called in the Old Testament the mountains of Ephraim.

(28) ΊΩΣΗΦ ΕΥΛΟΓΗΣΕΝ ΣΕ Ο ΘΕΟΣ ΕΥΛΟΓΙΑΝ ΓΗΣ ΕΧΟΥΣΗΣ

ΠΑΝΤΑ˙ ΚΑΙ ΠΑΛΙΝ ΑΠ ЄΥΛΟΓΙΑC ΚΫ Η ΓΗ ΑΥΤΟΥ
Ἰωσὴφ εὐλόγησέν σε ὁ θεὸς εὐλογίαν γῆς ἐχούσης πάντα,
καὶ πάλιν ἀπ' εὐλογίας κ(υρίο)υ ἡ γῆ αὐτοῦ
Joseph, God blessed you with the blessing of the earth that possesses everything, and again: blessed of the Lord be his land
A combination of the two benedictions for Joseph from Gen. 49:25 and Deut. 33:13 according to the Greek Septuagint version, represented in red cubes on brownish ground.

(29) ΑΝΑ[ΤΟΛΙΚΟΝ ΟΡΙ]ΟΝ ΤΗC Ι'ΟΥΔΑΙΑC
Ἀνατολικὸν ὅριον τῆς Ἰουδαίας
The eastern border of Judaea
The text is quoted from *Eus.On.* 14:7 who erroneously combined the Scorpion Pass (*Ma^{c}alē ^{c}Aqrabbīm* Numb. 34:3) southwest of the Dead Sea with the northern Aqrabim (= present ^{c}*Aqraba*, coord. 182-170), about 11 km southeast of *Nāblus*. Eusebius was probably influenced by Fl. Josephus, *Jewish War* III:3:5 (§ 55) who classes the northern Aqrabim (Akrabeta) among the districts of Herodian Judaea.

(30) [ΑΚ]ΡΑΒΙΜ˙Η ΝΥ[Ν ΑΚ]ΡΑΒΙΤΤ[ΙΝΗ]
Ακραβιμ, ἡ νῦν Ακραβιττινη
Akrabim, now the Akrabittine
Eus.On. 14:7-12. The site is identical with ^{c}*Aqraba* (coord. 182-170), about 11 km southeast of *Nāblus*. The mosaicist confused the name of the village (Akrabim) with the district-name (Akrabittine) of Herodian and later times.

(31) [CΗΛ]Ω [......] Η ΚΙ[ΒΩΤΟC]
Σηλω ...... ἡ κιβωτός
Shiloh ... (there was once?) the Ark
I Sam. 3:3; 4:3-5 a.o.; *Eus.On.* 156:28-31; Fl. Josephus, *Antiquities* V:1:19 (§ 68); also mentioned by some Christian pilgrims. The site is identical with *Ḫirbat Sēlūn* (coord. 177-162) near *Turmus* ^{c}*Ayyā*, situated about 18 km south of *Nāblus* not far from the Jerusalem-*Nāblus* road, very much displaced on the Madaba map.

(32) ΝЄΑΠΟΛΙC
Νεάπολις
Neapolis
This is present *Nāblus*, founded in 73 A.D. by the Roman emperor Vespasianus and named *Colonia Flavia Neapolis*. The settlement was the Hellenistic-Roman-Byzantine successor of ancient Shechem (nr. 36). The

large representation of Neapolis is badly damaged. The following details are still visible (see F.-M. Abel, *RB 1923, p. 120-132*): parts of the wall with towers surrounding the city. From the eastern gate, flanked by two towers, a colonnaded street runs from east to west, the so-called Roman *cardo maximus* (= main street). This street seems to be crossed by a shorter one running from north to south. Left above the intersection we note a small building with a red dome on two columns, perhaps a public fountain, possibly at the place of the present *an-Naṣr* mosque. In the southern part of the city there is a strange semicircular object, looking like a theatre, but possibly being a Nymphaion at present *ᶜAyn Qaryūn* where indeed Roman remains have been discovered. The large church in the southeast might be the cathedral of Neapolis, attacked by the Samaritans in 484 A.D. Two towers, perhaps protecting another gate, are visible in the southeastern wall. From there the Samaritans were expected when they came down from Mount Gerizim (nr. 33).

(33) ΤΟΥΡ ΓΑΡΙΖΙΝ	Τουρ Γαριζιν	Mount Gerizim
ΤΟΥΡ ΓΩΒΗΛ	Τουρ Γωβηλ	Mount Ebal
ΓΑΡΙΖЄΙΝ	Γαριζειν	Gerizim
ΓЄΒΑΛ	Γεβαλ	Ebal

The famous mountains Gerizim (*Ǧabal aṭ-Ṭōr*) and Ebal (*Ǧabal Islāmīya*) are listed twice on the Madaba map: above and beneath the plain of *Nāblus*/Shechem and at the edge of the mountains northwest of Jericho. *Eus.On.* 64:9-17 locates them near Jericho, adding the following explanation: 'The Samaritans show other ones near Neapolis, but they are wrong, for the mountains shown by them are too far from each other, so that it is impossible to hear one's voice when calling to each other' (see Deut. 27). This is, however, an error. The Samaritans laid claim to these mountains, considering them to be their own holy mountains. Consequently, the orthodox Jews in Jerusalem and elsewhere felt forced to locate the Biblical mountains at another spot; the Samaritans were not allowed to be right. Eusebius followed the orthodox Jewish tradition. The mosaic artist preferred a Solomonic solution: he listed the mountains twice, indicating by larger letters that he regarded their location near Neapolis as being correct.

(34) [CY]ΧΑΡ Η ΝΥΝ [C]ΥΧΩΡΑ

Συχαρ ἡ νῦν Συχωρα

Sychar, now Sychora

Gospel of John 4:5f.; *Eus.On.* 164:1-4; also mentioned by some Christian pilgrims and by the Early Fathers, mainly in their commentaries on the Gospel of John. The village is identical with *al-ᶜAskar* (coord. 177-180) east of *Nāblus*.

35 ΤΟ ΤΟΥ ΙѠϹΗΦ

Τὸ τοῦ 'Ιωσήφ

(The Tomb) of Joseph

Gen. 33:18-20; Josh. 24:32; Gospel of John 4:6; *Eus.On.* 54:23-24; also mentioned by Jewish, Christian and Muslim authors. The site is identical with present *Qabr an-Nabī Yūsuf* (coord. 177-180) east of ancient Shechem (nr. 36).

36 ϹΥΧЄΜ Η Κ͵ ϹΙΚΙΜΑ Κ͵ ϹΑΛΗΜ

Συχεμ ἡ κ(αὶ) Σικιμα κ(αὶ) Σαλημ

Shechem, also Sikima and Salem

The text is almost literally quoted from *Eus.On.* 150:1-7. The famous city, often mentioned in the Old Testament and elsewhere, is identical with *Tall Balāṭa* (coord. 176-180) east of *Nāblus*. The name Salem is taken from Gen. 14:18. The enigmatic city of Melchizedek, 'king of Salem' and 'priest of God Most High' , has been identified with Shechem, with Salumias south of Skythopolis (nr. 3) and, of course, with Jerusalem. There is, indeed, a village called *Sālim* (coord. 181-179), 4 km east of ancient Shechem. The mosaicist, following Eusebius against most ancient authors, distinguishes between Shechem and Neapolis, although *Tall Balāṭa* was scarcely populated in Byzantine times.

37 ΟΠΟΥ Η ΠΗΓΗ ΤΟΥ ΪΑΚѠΒ

Ὅπου ἡ πηγὴ τοῦ 'Ιακώβ

Where Jacob's Well is

Gospel of John 4:5f.; mentioned by all Christian pilgrims and most of the Early Fathers, especially in their commentaries on the Gospel of John. The identity of this holy place is well established since the 4th century: *Bīr Yaᶜqūb* (coord. 177-179) at *Balāṭa*, southeast of ancient Shechem. The church represented on the map was built around 380 at the latest and is first mentioned by St. Jerome.

38 [ΔѠΘΑЄΙΜ ЄΝΘΑ ЄΥΡЄΝ] ΙѠ[ϹΗΦ ΤΟΥϹ ΑΔЄΛΦΟΥϹ ΑΥΤΟΥ ΝЄΜΟ]Ν[ΤΑϹ]

Δωθαειμ ἔνθα εὗρεν 'Ιωσὴφ τοὺς ἀδελφοὺς αὐτοῦ νέμοντας

Dothaim where Joseph found his brothers pasturing

Gen. 37:17; the text is restored according to *Eus.On.* 76:13-15. The site is identical with *Tall Dōṯā* (coord. 172-202), about 8 km southwest of *Ǧanīn*. For the restoration of this long inscription from only two and a half letters (only on the original map, not on the drawing) see H. Donner, *ZDPV 83 (1967) p. 25-27*. Instead of the inscription the symbol of a small village is depicted erroneously on the sketch.

(39) [ΚΛΗΡΟC ЄΦΡ]ΑΙΜ

Κλῆρος Εφραιμ

The lot of Ephraim

The expression is derived from the Greek version of Josh. 13-19: the Biblical account according to which Joshua distributed the land among the Israelite tribes by casting lots.

(40) ΘЄΡΑCΠΙC

Θερασπις

Theraspis

An unknown village, the name of which is never attested in literary sources, neither in antiquity nor later on.

(41) ΒЄΝΙΑΜΙΝ CΚΙΑΖЄΙ Ο ΘC ЄΠ ΑΥΤΩ ΚΑΙ ΑΝΑ ΜЄCΟΝ ΤΩΝ ΟΡΙΩΝ ΑΥΤΟΥ ΚΑΤЄΠΑΥCЄΝ

Βενιαμιν σκιάζει ὁ θ(εὸ)ς ἐπ᾿αὐτῷ καὶ ἀνὰ μέσον τῶν ὀρίων αὐτοῦ κατέπαυσεν

Benjamin, God shields him and dwells in between his mountains

The text of this benediction, written in white letters on black background, is quoted from Deut. 33:12 according to the Greek Septuagint version. The Septuagint, however, reads 'in between his shoulders', not taking into consideration that the Hebrew expression 'his shoulders' metaphorically means 'his mountain slopes'. The mosaicist interpreted the text geographically correctly, emending the Septuagint.

(42) ΚΛΗΡ[ΟC ΒЄΝΙΑΜΙΝ]

Κλῆρος Βενιαμιν

The lot of Benjamin

For this expression see nr. 39. Jerusalem was classed with Benjamin by the Old Testament (Josh. 15:8; 18:16-21; Judg. 1:21) and *Eus.On.* 106:1.

(43) ЄΦΡΩΝ Η ЄΦΡΑΙΑ ЄΝΘΑ ΗΛΘЄΝ Ο ΚC :

Εφρων ἡ Εφραια ἔνθα ἦλθεν ὁ κ(ύριο)ς

Ephron which is Ephraia where the Lord walked

Gospel of John 11:54; *Eus.On.* 90:18f. and 28:4f.; Fl. Josephus, *Jewish*

War IV:9:9 (§ 551). The site is identical with *aṭ-Ṭayyiba* (coord. 178-151), about 5 km northeast of *Bētīn*. The Aramaic form Ephraia is used by St. Jerome in his translation of *Eus.On.* 86:1f. (87:1f.).

(44) ΡЄΜΜѠΝ

Ρεμμων

Remmon (= Rimmon)

Eus.On. 144:11f. It is identical with *ar-Rammūn* (coord. 178-148), 5.5 km east of *Bētīn*.

(45) ΛȣΖΑ· ΗΚΑΙ ΒЄΘΗΛ

Λουζα, ἡ καὶ Βεθηλ

Luz(a), also Bethel

Gen. 28:10-22; 35:1-15; *Eus.On.* 40:20-24 and 120:8-10; also mentioned by some Christian pilgrims and Early Fathers. It is modern *Bētīn* (coord. 172-148). Bethel, whose oldest name was Luz, is situated on the ancient road from Jerusalem to Neapolis. On the Madaba map it is represented much too far to the east, certainly from lack of space. The road is shown in white cubes going right across the benediction for Benjamin (nr. 41).

(46) ϹΑ[. . . .

Σα[...

Sa...

Remains of a name which cannot be restored.

(47) ΑΙΛΑΜѠΝ ЄΝΘΑ ЄϹΤΗ ϹЄΛΗΝΗ ЄΠΙ Τȣ ΝΑΥΗ

Ι̅Ϲ̣ [ΜΙΑ]Ν ЄΜΗΡ̣[ΑΝ]

Αιλαμων ἔνθα ἔστη ἡ σελήνη ἐπὶ τοῦ Ναυη Ι(ησου)ς μίαν ἐμήραν (= ἡμέραν)

Ailamon where stood the moon in the time of Joshua, son of Nun, one day

Josh. 10:12-13; *Eus.On.* 18:13-16. Here the Biblical village of Aijalon is under discussion. The Greek transliterations vary slightly; the form Ailamon is peculiar to the Madaba map. Aijalon was not situated east of Bethel, as Eusebius states, followed by the mosaicist, but near Nikopolis (modern *ᶜAmwās*): it is identical with the now completely destroyed village *Yālō* (coord. 152-138). The correct location was known in Byzantine times, for example by St. Jerome and others. The mosaicist, however, did not take notice of it.

(48) ΓΟΦΝΑ

Γοφνα

Gophna

Fl. Josephus, *Jewish War* III:3:5 (§ 54f.); *Eus.On.* 168:16, not attested in the Bible. The village is identical with *Ǧifnā* (coord. 170-152), 6 km north of *al-Bīra*. *Ǧifnā* is situated north, not southeast of *ar-Rām* (nr. 49) and *al-Ǧīb* (nr. 50); it is displaced on the map.

(49) ΡΑΜΑ

Ραμα

Rama

I Sam. 7:17; 8:14; *Eus.On.* 144:14f. The village is identical with *ar-Rām* (coord. 172-140) north of Jerusalem on the road to Neapolis (*Nāblus*).

(50) ΓΑΒΑΩΝ

Γαβαων

Gabaon (= Gibeon)

Josh. 9; I Kings 3:4-15; *Eus.On.* 66:11-16. The village is identical with *al-Ǧīb* (coord. 167-139), about 9 km northwest of Jerusalem, situated on the road to Nikopolis (*ᶜAmwās*, nr. 73) and Lydda/Diospolis (*Ludd*, nr. 61). On the map it is shown too far to the east.

(51) ΑΡΜΑΘΕΜ Η ΑΡΙΜΑΘΕΑ

Αρμαθεμ ἡ Αριμαθεα

Armathem (= Ramathaim) which is Arimathea

I Sam. 1:1; I Macc. 11:34; Matth. 27:57; Mark 15:43; Luke 23:51; John 19:38; *Eus.On.* 32:21-23 and 144:27-29. Identification and location are doubtful. Ramathaim is the birthplace of the prophet Samuel, Arimathea or Arimathia the town of Joseph who placed the Lord's body in his own tomb. Eusebius identified both villages, followed by the mosaicist, and located Arimathea correctly at *Rantīs* (coord. 151-159), 14 km northeast of Diospolis (Lydda, modern *Ludd*). This location, however, cannot be meant on the Madaba map, because Diospolis (nr. 61) is represented too far away. Since the 6th century at the latest, Christian pilgrims found the Ramathaim of Samuel on *an-Nabī Samwīl* (coord. 167-137), about 7 km northwest of Jerusalem, the *mons gaudii* ('mountain of joy') of the Crusaders. Here the traditional tomb of Samuel is still shown. Should we not consider this location, not far from Rama and Gibeon, for the mosaic map as well? It is separated from Jerusalem only by the benediction for Benjamin (nr. 41) and should have been placed more to the west – but there we read the benediction for Joseph (nr. 28).

(52) ΓΗΘϹ[ΙΜΑΝΗ]

Γηθσιμανη

Gethsemane

Matth. 26:36ff.; Mark 14:32ff.; Luke 22:39ff.; John 18:1ff.; *Eus.On.* 74:16-18; also mentioned by all Christian pilgrims. It is the place beyond the Kidron Valley where Jesus prayed and was betrayed by Judas Iscariot. The little church on the left is first mentioned by St. Jerome and by the nun Etheria (*ecclesia elegans* 'the beautiful church').

(53) ΤΟ ΤЄΤΑΡΤΟΝ

Τὸ τέταρτον

The fourth milestone

A road station on the 4th mile of the road from Jerusalem to Nikopolis (*ᶜAmwās*) and Diospolis (Lydda, *Ludd*). Road stations of such kind, represented here as a very small village, are called in Latin either *mansio* ('place for spending the night') or *mutatio* ('place for changing the horses'). The station might be identified with *Ḫirbat al-Hawānīt*.

(54) ΤΟ ЄΝΝΑ

Τὸ ἔννα<τον>

The ninth milestone

Another road station on the 9th mile of the road mentioned above (see nr. 53), possibly identical with *Ḫirbat al-Latātīn*.

(55) ΒЄΘѠΡѠΝ

Βεθωρων

Bethoron

Josh. 10:10f.; I Kings 9:17; I Macc. 3:16ff.; Fl. Josephus, *Jewish War* II: 19:1 (§ 516); *Eus.On.* 46:21-25. The site is identical with *Bēt ᶜŪr al-fōqa* (coord. 160-143) and *at-taḥta* (coord. 158-144), both villages being separated by the famous 'descent of Bethoron', often mentioned in the Bible and elsewhere. The villages are represented on the Madaba map by a single symbol beneath the inscription. The steplike dark cubes right of it might be an indication of the 'descent'.

(56) ΚΑ[...]ЄΡȣΤΑ

Κα...ερουτα

Ka...eruta

Remains of a name, damaged and roughly repaired, which cannot be restored (see H. Donner, *ZDPV 81, 1965, p. 44-46*).

(57) ΜⲰΔЄЄΙΜ· Η ΝΥΝ ΜⲰΔΙΘΑ· ЄΚ ΤΑΥΤΗⲤ ΗⲤΑΝ ΟΙ ΜΑΚΚΑΒΑΙΟΙ

Μωδεειμ, ἡ νῦν Μωδιθα, ἐκ ταύτης ἦσαν οἱ Μακκαβαίοι
Modeïm, now Moditha, whence were the Maccabees

I Macc. 2:1; *Eus.On.* 132:16f. (from where the text is taken almost literally). The ancient village is identical with *ar-Rās* near *al-Midya* (coord. 150-149), about 12 km east of *ar-Ramla*.

(58) ΑΔΙΑΘΙΜ Η ΝΥΝ ΑΔΙΘΑ

Αδιαθιμ ἡ νῦν Αδιθα
Adiathim, now Aditha

I Macc. 12:38; 13:13; Fl. Josephus, *Antiquities* XIII:6:4 (§ 203); *Eus.On.* 24:24f. The village is identical with *al-Ḥadīṯa* (coord. 145-152), 5 km east of *Ludd* (Lydda, Diospolis).

(59) ΒЄΤΟΜЄΛΓЄΖΙⲤ

Βετομελγεζις
Betomelgezis

An unknown village, the name of which does not occur in any literary source.

(60) ....]ΙΡΑ

...ιρα
...ira

Remains of a name which cannot be restored (certainly ...ira, not ...ora as some scholars suggested).

(61) ΛⲰΔ· ΗΤΟΙ ΛΥΔЄΑ Η Κ∽ ΔΙΟⲤΠΟΛΙⲤ

Λωδ, ἤτοι Λυδεα ἡ κ(αὶ) Διόσπολις
Lod, also Lydea, also Diospolis

This is ancient Lod (Lydda), named Diospolis by the Roman emperor Septimius Severus (193-211 A.D.), now *Ludd* (coord. 140-151). The city is often mentioned in different literary sources, mainly as the veneration centre of St. George (*al-Ḫaḍr*). The first one who speaks of the cult of St. George is the archdeacon Theodosius (between 518 and 530), ch. 4. According to Acts 9,32-43, St. Peter healed the paralytic Aeneas at Lydda and raised Tabitha-Dorcas from the dead at nearby Joppe. On the Madaba map, Lydda seems to be represented as an open city, without a wall. Two colonnaded streets are visible: the first one running from east to west and ending at a gate – if it is a gate and not the entrance of a building –, another one like a semicircle round the front of a large church, in all probability the basilica of St. George. The second church north of and parallel to the main street might have been devoted to St. Aeneas and St. Dorcas, although a church of these Saints is not attested in Byzantine literature. In the southern wall of the church just mentioned we note three pillars of white cubes: columns of another street parallel to the *cardo maximus*? One profane building is seen north of the northern church, and three houses clustered south of St. George's basilica.

(62) [CA]ΦAPЄA

Σαφαρεα

Sapharea

The village is not mentioned elsewhere in Byzantine literature, but is attested as Saphyria in the Crusaders' times. It is identical with *as-Sāfirīya* (coord. 136-155), about 5 km northwest of Lydda (Diospolis).

(63) [BЄ/HT]ỌΔЄΓANA

Βε/ητοδεγανα

Betodegana

Josh. 15:41; *Eus.On.* 50:15f. The name traces back to Canaanite *Bēt-Dāgōn* 'the house (= temple) of the god Dagon' who was venerated by the Philistines. The site is probably identical with *Bēt Dağan*, about 6 km northwest of Lydda (Diospolis). The gable of a church is seen inside the village.

(64) [KΛH]POC ΔAN

Κλῆρος Δαν

The lot of Dan

For this expression see nr. 39. Here the first settlement area of the Danites is meant (Josh. 19:40-46), before the tribe migrated to the north, captured the city of Laish and named it Dan (*Tall al-Qāḍī* near *Bānyās*) according to Judg. 17-18.

(65) [I]NA TI ΠAPOI[KЄI ΠΛ]OIOIC

Ἵνα τὶ παροικεῖ πλοίοις

Why does he (Dan) remain in ships?

This text is quoted from Judg. 5:17 according to the Greek Septuagint version. The song of Deborah seems to refer to the Phoenician merchant marine; the mosaicist, however, thinks of the Mediterranean which is nearby. He put this phrase at the first tribal area of Dan, although Judg. 5:17 presumes the second one (see nr. 64).

(66) ΤΟ ΤȢ ΑΓΙȢ ΙΩΝΑ

Τὸ τοῦ ἁγίου Ιωνα

(The sanctuary) of St. Jonah

A memorial building, similar to nr. 24, with a red dome flanked by two towers. It is one of several memorial places recalling the prophet Jonah's being vomited onto dry land by the fish (Jonah 2:10). The most important ones are: *an-Nabī Yūnus* near *Ṣarafand* southwest of ancient Sidon (*Ṣaydā*); *Tall Yūnis*, 5 km south of *Yāfā*; *an-Nabī Yūnis* (coord. 116-135), 4 km northeast of *Mīnat Asdūd*, the ancient harbour of Ashdod (nr. 90); *Ḫān Yūnis* (coord. 083-083) southwest of Gaza (nr. 118). All of them are situated near the seashore. On the Madaba map, probably *Tall Yūnis* (coord. 124-156) near *Yāfā* is meant, for it seems to be too far from Ashdod harbour. The connection of the prophet Jonah with *Yāfā* might have been influenced by the famous myth of Perseus, Andromeda and the monster whose bones were shown in the harbour of *Yāfā*. The brownish round object in the sea beneath the sanctuary of Jonah, however, is hardly part of Jonah's fish - as often suggested -, but rather the bow or the stern of a ship.

(67) ΕΝΕΤΑΒΑ

Ενεταβα

Enetaba

An unidentified village, mentioned in Rabbinical literature, the name of which means 'good spring'. Could it be *Ḫirbat Kafr Ṭāb*, about 4 km east of *ar-Ramla*? If so, the representation would be displaced on the map.

(68) ΓΕΘ· Η ΝΥΝ ΓΙΤΤΑ ΜΙΑ ΠΟΤΕ ΤΩΝ Ε̄ ϹΑΤΡΑΠΙΩΝ

Γεθ, ἡ νῦν Γιττα μία πότε τῶν πέντε σατραπίων

Geth (= Gath), now Gitta, formerly one of the five satrapies

The Biblical city of Gath, now *Tall aṣ-Ṣāfī* (coord. 135-123) about 18 km east-southeast of Ashdod, is obviously meant here. Its location, however, is wrong, for it is represented north of Ashdod. The mosaicist followed *Eus.On.* 72:2-4 where another Geth is mentioned, also called Gitthaim or Gittham, identical with *Rās Abū Ḥamīd* southeast of *ar-Ramla*, or less probably, with *as-Sāqīya* 8 km east-southeast of *Yāfā*. The mosaicist ignored the better location in *Eus.On.* 68:4-7. The 'five satrapies' are the Philistine city territories often mentioned in the Bible: Gaza (*Ġazza*), Ashkelon (*ᶜAsqalān*), Ashdod (*Asdūd*), Ekron (*Ḫirbat al-Muqannaᶜ*), and Gath. The text is derived from Eusebius' description of other members of the Philistine confederacy (*Eus.On.* 22:7.11.16).

(69) ·Ι·ΑΒΝΗΛ· Η ΚΑΙ ·Ι·ΑΜΝΙΑ

Ιαβνηλ, ἡ καὶ Ιαμνια

Jabneel, also Jamnia

Josh. 15:11; *Eus.On.* 106:20f. It is identical with *Yibnā* (coord. 126-141), about 12 km northeast of Ashdod. Jamnia was the residence of the Jewish Synhedrium after 70 A.D.; it is often mentioned in Jewish and other literary sources. It also became the centre of Jewish erudition, the place of famous teachers like Rabbi Gamaliel and Rabbi Jochanan ben Zakkai. After 135 Jamnia had a Samaritan congregation with a synagogue. It was christianized in the 4th century. The representation shows an unwalled city with three ecclesiastical buildings (red roofs). The central one, with steps leading to the front entrance, is probably the main church of St. Stephanus and St. Thomas, built by the empress Eudocia around 440 and mentioned by Petrus the Iberian (Raabe 114f.). This church was situated on the top of the present *Tall*, rebuilt in Crusaders' times and followed by a mosque, the minaret of which, originating in the 14th century, is still preserved. The other ecclesiastical buildings with flat roofs, in the north and south, are not identified. Formerly, there was a memorial edifice above the tomb of *Abū Ḥurēra*, one of the Prophet's companions, now destroyed, which in the Middle Ages was believed to belong to Rabbi Gamaliel. This was, however, not a Christian memorial place, and was situated in the west of the present *Tall*.

(70) ΑΚΕΛΔΑΜΑ

Ακελδαμα

Akeldama

This is the 'field of blood' (Acts 1:19), bought with the 30 silver coins of Judas Iscariot (Matth. 27:6-8). The mosaicist seems to have followed *Eus.On.* 38:20f. who wrongly located the place 'north of Mount Zion', but corrected himself in 102:14-16 and was corrected by St. Jerome. The real Akeldama (*Dēr Abū Ṭōr*), mentioned by nearly all Christian pilgrims and Early Fathers, is situated in the Valley of Hinnom (*Wādi ar-Rabāba*) south of Jerusalem. It was for a long time a cemetery for pilgrims.

(71) ΘΑΜΝΑ ΕΝΘΑ ΕΚΕΙΡΕΝ ·Ι·ΟΥΔΑΣ ΤΑ ΑΥΤΟΥ ΠΡΟΒΑΤΑ·

Θαμνα ἔνθα ἔκειρεν Ιουδας τὰ αὐτοῦ πρόβατα

Thamna (= Thimna) where Judah sheared his sheep

Gen. 38:12f.; *Eus.On.* 96:24-26 from which the text is quoted. Biblical Thimna is most probably identical with *Tall Baṭāšī* (coord. 141-132). The location does not agree, however, with the representation on the Madaba map, for Thamna is shown north of Nikopolis (*ᶜAmwās*). The mosaicist obviously suffered from lack of space: he wanted to give a large representation of the famous Nikopolis and put it too much to the south.

(72) ANΩB H NYN BHTOANNABA·

Ανωβ ἡ νῦν Βητοανναβα

Anob, now Betoannaba

Eus.On. 20:15-17. The problem of locating is difficult. According to Eusebius (4 miles east of Diospolis) the village of ᶜ*Annāba* (coord. 145-145) comes into question, situated about 6 km southeast of Lydda (Diospolis, *Ludd*). St. Jerome, however, mentions another 'Bethannaba', 8 miles east of Diospolis, which is surely identical with *Bēt Nūba* (coord. 153-140), situated 4 km northeast of Nikopolis (ᶜ*Amwās*). The problem is unsolved. The first location seems to be better, but we have to take into consideration that Nikopolis is represented too far to the south and that, consequently, all cities and villages in that area are displaced.

(73) NIKOΠOΛIC

Νικόπολις

Nikopolis

Luke 24:13; *Eus.On.* 90:15-17; also mentioned by nearly all Christian pilgrims and Early Fathers, and in other sources as well. The site is identical with present ᶜ*Amwās* (coord. 149-138). Biblical Emmaus was named Nikopolis by the Roman emperor Heliogabalus in 220/1 A.D. It is difficult to interpret the representation. The city seems to be walled up, with three or more towers and some gates belonging either to the wall or to peculiar buildings. The church in the center of the city is certainly the basilica, built earlier than 529 and destroyed - to what extent? - by the Samaritans in 529. The emperor Justinian built a smaller church immediately north of it. Is it identical with the red-roofed building in the northern edge of the representation? It is not quite definite whether the basilica was dedicated to St. Cleopas - or even built above the place of his supposed house. The southern church - or two churches? - is unknown and unidentified. For all these problems see H. Vincent - F.-M. Abel, *Emmaus, sa basilique et son histoire* (1932).

(74) ΓΕΔΟΥΡ· H Kϛ ΓΙΔΙΡΘΑ

Γεδουρ ἡ κ(αὶ) Γιδιρθα

Gedur, also Gidirtha

This is another difficult locating problem. *Eus.On.* 68:22f. mentions a village called Gedur, in his time Gedrus, 10 miles on the road from Diospolis (Lydda) to Eleutheropolis (*Bēt Ǧibrīn*, nr. 87): this 'very large' village might be identified with *Ḫirbat aš-Šēḫ* ᶜ*Alī Ǧadir* (coord. 146-137), 2.5 km west of *Laṭrūn*, i.e. not far from Nikopolis (nr. 73). Eusebius intends to explain the Gedor of Josh. 15:58 which is, however, situated more in the south, identical with *Ḫirbat Ǧadūr* (coord. 158-115), about 6 km north-northwest of *Ḥalḥūl* (coord. 160-109). The village Gedur or Gedera, in Aramaic Gidirtha, near *Laṭrūn* has no Biblical reference. Moreover, it is in relation to Nikopolis (*ᶜAmwās*), whereas the other villages in this area are represented regardless of Nikopolis. We may wonder if the mosaicist confused it with Gezer, in Greek Gazer or Gazera, identical with *Tall Ğezer* (coord. 142-140) near *Abū Šūša*, the well-known Biblical city (Josh. 10:33; Judg. 1:29; II Sam. 5:25; I Kings 9:15-17 a.o.). Otherwise, the absence of Gezer on the Madaba map would be rather odd because of its Biblical importance.

(75) ЄΦΡΑΘΑ

Εφραθα

Ephratha

Reference is here to the famous tomb of Rachel (coord. 169-125), identified since the 4th century as lying near Bethlehem and mentioned by nearly all Christian pilgrims and Early Fathers, and in Jewish and Muslim sources as well.

(76) ΡΑΜΑ˙ ΦѠΝΗ ЄΝ ΡΑΜΑ ΗΚȣCΘΗ

Ραμα, φωνὴ ἐν Ραμα ἠκούσθη

Rama, a voice was heard in Rama

Jerem. 31:15; Matth. 2:18 (literal quotation); *Eus.On.* 147:28-148:2. The tomb of Rachel was originally situated near Rama (*ar-Rām*, nr. 49) north of Jerusalem. The name Ephrat, mentioned in Gen. 35:19 was also the name of king David's family (Micah 5:1). This caused its transfer to the vicinity of Bethlehem which was known as David's birthplace. This transfer occured before the New Testament was written. Consequently, a village called Rama was supposed to exist near Bethlehem, and this assumption was supported by the very existence of a small Roman-Byzantine village at modern *Rāmat Rāḥēl*. Around 450 a church was built there, the so-called 'church of Kathisma' recalling Maria's resting on her way to Bethlehem. Instead of the church the non-existant village of Rama is represented on the Madaba map.

(77) ΒΗΘΛЄЄΜ

Βηθλεεμ

Bethlehem

Eus.On. 42:10-13; 82:10-14. The famous Biblical city, the birthplace of David and of Jesus Christ, is situated in a plain which is called by Eusebius 'hippodrome'. The mosaicist represented this plain with white cubes round the city and the red inscription. Strangely enough, the representation of the city itself is much smaller than that of other less important cities, e.g. Nikopolis, Lydda etc. Only the basilica of the Nativity is shown, built by the emperor Constantine and rebuilt after the earthquake of 510 by Justinian, with a red-roofed annex in the north, possibly the monastery of St. Paula. The wall, also restored under Justinian, is seen with one gate and one tower. Bethlehem was often visited and described, mainly by Christian pilgrims and by the Early Fathers. We know that there were many churches and memorial places, all ignored by the mosaicist. The reason why he did so is unknown.

(78) [ΚΛΗΡΟϹ] ΙΟΥΔΑ

Κλῆρος Ιουδα

The lot of Judah

For this expression see nr. 39.

(79) [Θ]ЄΚΟΥЄ

Θεκουε

Thekue (= Thekoa)

Am. 1:1; Jerem. 6:1; II Sam. 14:2; *Eus.On.* 86:12-14; also mentioned by Christian and Jewish authors as the birthplace of the prophet Amos. The village is identical with *Ḫirbat Tqū*^{c} (coord. 170-115), 8 km south of Bethlehem. On the left below the representation we notice the remains of a church with red roof: most likely the memorial church above the tomb of Amos, mentioned by Eusebius and other Christian authors. Church and village are similarly separated in Bethzachar (nr. 84) and Morasthi (nr. 86).

(80) ΒЄΘϹȣΡΑ

Βεθσουρα

Bethsura (= Bethzur)

Eus.On. 52:1-5; often mentioned by Christian authors in connection with St. Philipp's Fountain (nr. 81). It is identical with *Ḫirbat Burğ aṣ-Ṣūr* (coord. 159-110) northwest of *Ḥalḥūl*. Nearby *Ḫirbat aṭ-Ṭubēqa* is the older settlement from Old Testament, Hellenistic and Roman times.

(81) ΤΟ Τȣ ΑΓ< ΦΙΛΙΠΠΟΥ ЄΝΘΑ ΛЄΓȣϹΙ ΒΑΠΤΙϹΘΗΝΑΙ ΚΑΝΔΑΚΗΝ ΤΟΝ ЄΥΝΟΥΧΟΝ

Τὸ τοῦ ἁγί(ου) Φιλίππου ἔνθα λέγουσι βαπτισθῆναι Κανδάκην τὸν εὐνοῦχον

(The sanctuary) of St. Philipp where Candace the eunuch is said to have been baptized

Acts 8:26-39; *Eus.On.* 52:1-5. The place is identical with ^{c}*Ayn aḏ-Ḏirwa* (coord. 160-110) near *Ḥalḥūl.* A basilica is shown, and outside of it the round pool of St. Philipp's Fountain. The remains on the spot correspond exactly to this representation: the fountain is situated less than 50 m northwest of the ruins of the church which have almost totally disappeared. It is interesting to note how the mosaicist followed Eusebius and misunderstood him. The anonymous Ethiopian of Acts 8 was a eunuch of the queen Candace – this is quite clear from the New Testament text. Eusebius, however, only wrote ὁ εὐνοῦχος Κανδάκης 'the eunuch of Candace', omitting the word for queen. His text could be misinterpreted as if Candace were the eunuch's name – and the mosaicist fell into this trap, so did other Christian authors.

(82) [ΑΡΒѠ] Ḥ ΚΑΙ [ΤЄ]ṚЄΒΙΝΘΟC Η ΔΡỴ[C] ΜΑṂ[ΒΡΗ]

Αρβω ἡ καὶ τερέβινθος ἡ δρῦς Μαμβρη

Arbo, also the Terebinth

The oak of Mambre (= Mamre)

Gen. 18:1ff.; Fl. Josephus, *Jewish War* IV:9:7 (§ 533); *Eus.On.* 6:8-16 and 76:1-3; Sozomenos, *hist. eccl.* II:4 (PG 67,941); also mentioned by nearly all Christian pilgrims and other Christian, Jewish and Muslim authors. The site is identical with *Ḥaram Rāmat al-Ḫalīl* (coord. 160-107), 3 km north of Hebron (*al-Ḫalīl*). Arbo is Kirjath-Arba (Gen. 23:2), one of the names of ancient Hebron, and does not originally belong to Mamre but to the city of Hebron itself. The representation can be compared to the excavation results; see E. Mader, *Mambre. Die Ergebnisse der Ausgrabungen im Hl. Bezirk Râmet el-Ḫalîl in Südpalästina 1926-28* (1957). We see the basilica, built by the emperor Constantine around 330, destroyed by the Persians under Chosroes II in 614. North of it there is a red-roofed building, seemingly in two storeys, the upper one colonnaded. Is it an indication of the *temenos* wall, erected by the Roman emperor Hadrian – for Mamre has a remarkable pre-Christian history – and renewed by Constantine? In this case the basilica, situated within the holy area in the east, is put outside in order to make it visible. There are, however, no literary or archaeological traces of columns upon the big square stones of the wall. Or did the mosaicist intend to indicate the annexes of the basilica or even a monastery? On the right side Abraham's sacred tree is shown: the terebinth or oak, standing immediately beside Abraham's well, not represented here. The fragmentarily preserved church south of it does not belong to Mamre, although it is beneath the inscription 'the oak of Mamre', but to Hebron itself: it is the Byzantine church of the Patriarchal tombs, above the cave of Machpelah (Gen. 23), at *Ḥaram al-Ḫalīl*. The image of the city of Hebron, to the south, is lost.

(83) CWXW

Σωχω

Socho

Eus.On. 156:18-20; John Moschus, *Pratum Spirituale* 180 (PG 87,3052). The site is identical with *Ḫirbat ᶜAbbād* (coord. 148-120), 3 km southeast of *Zakarīya*. Nearby *Ḫirbat aš-Šuwēka* from early Arab times, preserves the ancient name. The village of Socho is displaced on the Madaba map.

(84) ΒΕΘΖΑΧΑΡ ΤΟ ΤΟΥ ΑΓΙΟΥ ΖΑΧΑΡΙΟΥ

Βεθζαχαρ τὸ τοῦ ἁγίου Ζαχαριου

Bethzachar

(The sanctuary) of St. Zacharias

Bethzachar(iah) is mentioned by some Christian authors, e.g. Sozomenos, *hist. eccl.* IX:17 (PG 67,1628f.; GCS 50,407f.) a.o. It is identical with *Zakarīya* (coord. 144-124), 12 km north of *Bēt Ǧibrīn*, the ancient Eleutheropolis (nr. 87). During the Synod of Lydda in 415, the bones of the prophet Zechariah were found at *Kafr Zakarīya*, and they produced a specific Christian holy place and cult. In the following times the Christian tradition mixed three persons called Zechariah (Zacharias): the Old Testament prophet, the High Priest of II Chron. 24:20-22 who was killed by king Joash (Matth. 23:35), and the father of St. John the Baptist (Luke 1:5). The representation is very interesting. On the left, we see a medium-sized symbol of a village with three towers. On the right, separated from the village and seemingly outside of it, there is the sanctuary of St. Zacharias: a red-roofed colonnaded portico (or narthex), above it the façade of the church with three gates, and above that behind the church is a semicircular court surrounded by one more red-roofed portico. The tomb of the Saint was situated in the open court behind the basilica attached to it, usually called Martyrium. The next parallel to this representation we find in Jerusalem: the church of Holy Sepulchre (section D, nr. 7). It is interesting to see that the mosaicist did not depict the basilica in the usual manner: not looking askance at it, but to the front of it, and omitting the nave and the roof. West of Socho (nr. 83) and northwest of Bethzachar there is an unnamed village in the mountains: a representation of Biblical Aseka (*Tall Zakarīya*, coord. 144-123) as described by *Eus.On.* 18:10-12?

(85) CΑΦΙΘΑ

Σαφιθα

Saphitha

This Byzantine village is not attested in ancient literary sources. It was situated in the vicinity of *Tall aṣ-Ṣāfī*, the site of the Philistine Gath (nr. 68) and might be identified with *Ḫirbat aṣ-Ṣāfīya* (coord. 136-123), 1 km east-northeast of *Tall aṣ-Ṣāfī*. Its name, meaning 'the white one', is preserved in the Crusaders' fortress Blanchegarde upon *Tall aṣ-Ṣāfī*.

(86) ΜΟΡΑϹΘΙ· ΟΘΕΝ ΗΝ ΜΙΧΑΙΑϹ Ο ΠΡΟΦ
ΤΟ ΤΟ̣ [ΑΓΙΟΥ ΜΙΧΑΙΟΥ]

Μορασθι, ὅθεν ἦν Μιχαιας ὁ προφ(ήτης)
Τὸ τοῦ ἁγίου Μιχαιου
Morasthi, whence was the prophet Micah
(The sanctuary) of St. Micah

Micah 1:1.14; the text quoted from *Eus.On.* 134:10f.; also mentioned by Christian pilgrims and Early Fathers. The Byzantine Morasthi is identical with *Ḫirbat Umm al-Baṣal* (coord. 140-114), 1.5 km north of *Bēt Ǧibrīn* (Eleutheropolis, nr. 87) half-way to *Tall al-Ǧudēda*, the site of ancient Moreshet-Gath. The memorial church of the prophet Micah above his tomb, first mentioned by St. Jerome (Pilgrimage of St. Paula and Eustochium, ch. 14), is separated from the village like in Bethzachar (nr. 84) and Thekoa (nr. 79).

(87) Ε̣[ΛΕΥΘΕΡΟΠΟΛΙϹ]

Ἐλευθερόπολις
Eleutheropolis

Identical with *Bēt Ǧibrīn* (coord. 140-112). The inscription is broken, save for four black cubes forming a curved line: the remains of a Epsilon. The representation is fragmentarily preserved. The city is walled, three towers are seen from inside. A street runs from north to south, curving to the west and again to the south, having a colonnade only in its central part. Another colonnade in the north seems to mark a by-street, coming from northeast and ending near the front of a basilica. Eleutheropolis was a bishop's see, often mentioned in ecclesiastical and administrative Byzantine sources. The dedication of the basilica is unknown. They may have been the two martyrs Zebinas and Petrus, mentioned by Eusebius (*Martyrs in Palestine*, ch. 9-10). In the centre of the city we note a building with a yellowish-white dome on four columns. Scholars have connected it with what the anonymous pilgrim of Piacenza described in ch. 32: 'From there we struck off from a side road and came to the city called Eleutheropolis, which is where Samson killed a thousand men with the jawbone of an ass, from which a spring came forth which to this day provides water for the whole area, for we also visited the place where it rises.' This report, however, does not have the air of describing a place inside the city. Moreover, the jawbone hill of Judg. 15: 14-19 seems to have been in the open fields, according to the Biblical account. Probably the domed building is nothing but a public fountain. It is flanked by two houses with sloped roofs, the right of which is red.

(88) ΑΚΚΑΡ̣[ωΝ] Η ΝΥΝ ΑΚΚ̣Α̣Ρ̣Α̣

Ακκαρων ἥ νῦν Ακκαρα

Akkaron (= Ekron), now Akkara

Josh. 13:3; Judg. 1:18; I Sam. 5:10; II Kings 1:2ff.; Jerem. 25:20; Am. 1:8; *Eus.On.* 22:6-10. Ekron was one of the Philistine city territories, identical with *Ḫirbat al-Muqanna*[c] (coord. 136-131), 14 km southeast of *Yibnā* (Jamnia, nr. 69). The remains of the Byzantine village were found 300 m northwest of the *Ḫirba*.

(89) ΑCΔωΔ̣ [Η ΚΑΙ ΑΖω]Τ[ΟC]

Ασδωδ ἥ καὶ Αζωτος

Ashdod, also Azotos

Josh. 11:22; I Sam. 5:1; Is. 20:1; Jerem. 25:20; Am. 1:8; 3:9; *Eus.On.* 20:18-20 and 22:11-14. The site is identical with *Asdūd* (coord. 117-129). The inland Ashdod, one of the Philistine city territories, was obviously less important and smaller than the harbour of Ashdod was in Byzantine times. We note two red roofs between the towers, the traces of unknown and unidentified churches.

(90) ΑΖωΤΟC ΠΑΡΑΛΟ̣[C]

Αζωτος πάραλος

Azotos (= Ashdod) by the sea

This is the ancient harbour of Ashdod, identical with *Mīnat Asdūd* (coord. 114-131), also called *Mīnat al-Qal*[c]*a* (named after the *Castellum Beroardi* of the Crusaders). The fragmentary representation of this very important harbour city is difficult to interpret. We note a colonnaded street running from north to south, seemingly interrupted by the façade of a church to which steps lead from the shore. Another ecclesiastical red-roofed building is seen north of this church; a third one has a yellowish triangular pediment and is in the south directly at the shore. The details are complicated by several clustered houses in between. These buildings cannot be identified, due to lack of literary information.

(91) ΑCΚΑΛω̣[Ν]

Ασκαλων

Ashkelon

Judg. 1:18; 14:19; I Sam. 6:17; Jerem. 25:20; Am. 1:8; *Eus.On.* 22:15-18; also mentioned by other Jewish, Christian and Muslim authors. Ancient Ashkelon, one of the Philistine city territories, is identical with [c]*Asqalān* (coord. 106-118). The preserved section of the representation shows that part of Byzantine Ashkelon which was surrounded in the Middle Ages by the big semicircular Crusaders' rampart. Parts of the wall are visible, with one tower on the left. Two other towers flank the eastern gate built in two storeys, the upper one showing a window. A broad square lies in front of the inner side of the eastern gate, from which two colonnaded streets run from east to west, similar to the situation inside the Damascus Gate in Jerusalem (section D, nr. 1). Between them is seen what has been interpreted as a rectangular pool, but is rather a house shown from above, with two windows. The left east-western street crosses another one going from north to south: at the intersection we see a yellowish dome, erected upon two columns – probably not a triumphal arch as is usually assumed, but a so-called *Tetrapylon* (of which only two columns are seen). The colonnaded street from north to south does not seem to extend beyond the right east-western street. A continuation, however, must have existed, perhaps beginning a little more to the west. West of the north-south street, between both east-west streets, a church is partly visible. Three profane buildings are shown in the northeastern part of the city. If we compare this representation to the town plan of ancient Ashkelon, we note a remarkable agreement. The eastern gate is the Jerusalem Gate (*Bāb al-Quds*) of the medieval city. The run of the streets corresponds approximately to that of medieval Ashkelon and to the present ways and paths on the *Tall*: from Jerusalem Gate to Sea Gate (*porta maris* of the Crusaders), from *Yāfā* Gate to Gaza Gate. The separation of two east-west streets, indeed, begins just after the square near the so-called *Buleuterion* (senate building) in the very centre of the city. The strange building in between these streets, mentioned above, is certainly not the *Buleuterion*, because this building was transformed into a theatre in the 5th century A.D. The church cannot be identified. Roman-Byzantine Ashkelon was famous for its beautiful wells (see Origenes, *Contra Celsum* IV:44). One of them has been described by the Piacenza pilgrim around 570 (ch. 33): 'Entering Ascalon we came to the very large Well of Peace, built like a theatre, in which one goes down by steps to the water.' Probably this well and perhaps other ones too were shown in the lost parts of the representation.

(82) [TO TΩ]Ṇ AIΓY[Π]ṬIΩN

Τὸ τῶν Αἰγυπτίων

(The sanctuary) of the Egyptians

Eusebius, *On the Martyrs in Palestine* X:1 (GCS Eus. II,2 [1908] p. 930); Anonymous Pilgrim of Piacenza, ch. 33. The Piacenza pilgrim mentions 'three brothers who were Egyptian martyrs. Each of them had a name of his own, but they are usually called the Egyptians.' Their sanctuary might be identical with one of the two Byzantine churches, unearthened in the quarter called *Barnea* in 1954 and 1966/7, about 2 km north of ancient Ashkelon.

III. Section C

This section shows two remarkable geographical features: the southern desert (the so-called *Negeb*) in white-yellowish cubes and the Nile Delta, the arms of which are also represented on a white-yellowish background. Furthest east we see a part of *Wādī 'l-ᶜArabā* south of the Dead Sea. Between *Wādī 'l-ᶜArabā* and the *Negeb* some mountain chains are represented: three on the left and one on the right. On the left we have the dislocation levels of the central Palestinian mountains towards the southern desert, very similar to the picture east of the Dead Sea (see above p. 36). The white interruptions between the mountain chains are not necessarily meaningful. In one of them, however, Mampsis (nr. 93) is situated, and this fact may lead to the conclusion that the mosaicist intended to indicate what is called in the Old Testament 'the Ascent of Scorpions' (Numb. 34:4; Josh. 15:3; Judg. 1:36): one of the ascents between *Wādī 'l-ᶜArabā* and the area of *ᶜArab as-Saᶜīdīya* and *ᶜArab aẓ-Ẓullām*, most probably *Naqb aṣ-Ṣafā* through which an ancient road ran down from Beersheba to the *ᶜArabā*. On the right we see another large mountain chain, possibly indicating the mountainous northern part of the Sinai peninsula, i.e. the area of *Ğabal al-Ḥalāl*, *Ğabal Yalaq*, *Ğabal al-Muġāra*, and *Ğabal ar-Rāḥa*. The Sinai itself was, of course, represented because of its Biblical importance, but is unfortunately lost.

In the west, a small fragment of the Mediterranean Sea is visible between Raphia and Pentaschoinon (nrs. 122 and 128). We note an interesting geographical inaccuracy: in reality, the coast-line turns westward south of Gaza, but on the Madaba map it turns east. The reason for this is clear. If the mosaicist had represented the coast-line correctly, he would have had to abandon the rectangular size of his map: the coast-line now going from top to bottom, and the Nile with its arms coming from the right side - completely impossible on a church floor! Moreover, a conflict would have been produced between real geography and religious geography. For in the ancient Christian tradition the Nile was one of the rivers of Paradise, and the Paradise was situated in the east according to Gen. 2: therefore the Nile had to run from the east to the west without any regard for the geographical facts, even though people may have known them. This is the explanation for the false geographical relation of Lower Egypt to Palestine.

The Nile Delta's representation is based on the oldest known description (Herodotus, *hist*. II:17:3-6) whose text runs as follows: 'The Nile, beginning from the Cataracts, divides Egypt into two parts as it flows to the sea. Now as far as the city Cercasorus the Nile flows in one channel, but after that it parts into three. One of these, which is called the Pelusian mouth, flows eastwards; the second flows westwards, and is called the Canobic mouth. But the direct channel of the Nile, when the river in its downward course reaches the sharp point of the Delta, flows thereafter clean through the middle of the Delta into the sea; in this is seen the greatest and most famous part of its waters, and it is called the Sebennytic mouth. There are also two channels which separate themselves from the Sebennytic and so flow into the sea, by name the Saïtic and the Mendesian. The Bolbitine and Bucolic mouths are not natural but dug channels' (translation by A.D. Godley, in the Loeb Classical Library, Herodotus II, p. 295).

The representation on the Madaba map corresponds exactly with this description. There are only three small differences: 1. The name Bolbytic on the map instead of Bolbitine in Herodotus' text is without any parallel. Probably it is only an error, or the mosaicist used another version of Herodotus than ours. 2. The mosaicist did not distinguish between the natural and the dug channels, the reason for which is clear: he wanted to draw the arms in the Delta symmetrically. There was no need to differ from Herodotus. He only had to interpret him, taking into consideration that Herodotus does not describe how and in what direction the arms run. 3. The Bucolic arm is lost, but it was still visible some decades ago as older photographs show. The Mendesian arm, mentioned by Herodotus, seems to be entirely absent. It can, however, easily be demonstrated that it originally was shown on the Madaba map. The inscription 'Sebennitic' (nr. 132) is completely preserved until the letter Y. Of the following letter T two white cubes still exist, forming part of a horizontal line, the cross-beam of the T. If this cross-beam is lengthened to the left, trying to restore the whole letter T, it becomes clear that the inscription together with the Sebennitic arm slightly deviated to the right. On the other hand, the left black limitation line of the arm moves slightly to the left. From these observations we have to conclude: another arm of the Nile, not preserved, branched off from the Sebennitic arm to the east, i.e. Herodotus' Mendesian arm. Thus, the mosaicist followed the tradition and got the magic total of seven mouths of the Nile.

We should not overlook the pleasing mosaic pictures in the Nile and its arms: a small boat, seven fish, and even the remains of a crocodile at the upper edge of the mosaic, the latter not depicted on the sketch. For the topographical peculiarities of Lower Egypt on the Madaba map see below p. 79-81.

(93) ΜΑΜΨΙC

Μαμψις

Mampsis

Eus.On. 8:8; also mentioned by other Byzantine authors and in inscriptions. The site, partly excavated in 1965-1967, is identical with *al-Kurnub* (coord. 156-048), about 37 km southeast of Beersheba. The representation shows a wide gate and the gable of a church (?). Mampsis is situated within the southern dislocation of the central Palestinian mountains towards the *Negeb*, shown by the mosaicist in a very impressive manner.

(94) ΠΡΑCΙΔΙΝ

Πρασιδιν

Prasidin (= Praesidium)

A Roman-Byzantine military post, mentioned in Byzantine administrative texts. It is identical with *Qaṣr al-Fēfa* (coord. 192-038), about 4 km south of *aṣ-Ṣāfī* in the *Ġōr aṣ-Ṣāfī*.

(95) ΘΑΜΑΡΑ

Θαμαρα

Thamara

Eus.On. 8:7-9. Another Roman-Byzantine military post and important road station, mentioned on the Peutinger Plates and in Byzantine administrative texts. It is most probably identical with ruins near *ᶜAyn al-ᶜArūs* (coord. 183-043), about 8 km southwest of the Dead Sea (S. Mittmann, *ZDPV* 93, 1977, p. 228-232).

(96) ΜΩΑ

Μωα

Moa

A third Roman-Byzantine military post, mentioned in the so-called Beersheba edict. It is probably to be identified with ruins in the area of *Moya ᶜAwād*, about 32 km west-southwest of *Fēnān*. No Byzantine remains have as yet been found there.

(97) ЄΡΗΜΟC CΙΝ ΟΠΟΥ ΚΑΤЄΠЄΜΦΘΗ ΤΟ ΜΑΝΝΑ

Ϗ Η ΟΡΤΥΓΟΜΗΤΡΑ

Ἐρῆμος Σιν ὅπου κατεπέμφθη τὸ μάννα κ(αὶ) ἡ ὀρτυγομήτρα

The Wilderness of Sin where the manna and the quails were sent down

This text refers to Exod. 16:1-36 and Numb. 11:4-34.

(98) ΡΑΦΙΔΙΜ· ЄΝΘΑ ЄΠЄΛΘΟΝΤΙ ΤѠ ΑΜΑΛΗΚ Ο ΙϹΡΑΗΛ ЄΠΟΛЄΜΗϹЄΝ

Ραφιδιμ, ἔνθα ἐπελθόντι τῷ Αμαληκ ὁ Ισραηλ ἐπολέμησεν

Raphidim, where Israel fought against the approaching Amalek

This text refers to Exod. 17:8-16; see *Eus.On.* 142:22-25. The location of Raphidim (Exod. 17:1.8) is unknown. Eusebius locates it not far from Mount Horeb and near Pharan which is historically *Wādī Fērān* in the Sinai peninsula. The mosaicist, however, apparently thinks of a place much nearer Palestine, perhaps in the southern desert (*Negeb*). A symbol for a village is missing, because Raphidim is described as a site, not an inhabited place (Petrus Diaconus, *CSEL* 39,118).

(99) ΒΗΡϹΑΒЄЄ Η ΝΥΝ ΒΗΡΟϹϹΑΒΑ· ЄѠϹ ΤΑΥΤΗϹ ΤΑ ΟΡΙΑ ΤΗϹ ΙΟΥΔΑΙΑϹ ΤΑ ΠΡΟϹ ΝΟΤΟΝ ΑΠΟ ΔΑΝ· ΤΗϹ ΠΡΟϹ ΠΑΝЄΑΔΙ ΗΤΙϹ ΟΡΙΖЄΙ ΤΑ ΠΡΟϹ ΒΟΡΡΑΝ

Βηρσαβεε ἡ νῦν Βηροσσαβα, ἕως ταύτης τὰ ὅρια τῆς Ἰουδαίας τὰ πρὸς νότον ἀπὸ Δαν, τῆς πρὸς Πανεάδι ἥτις ὁρίζει τὰ πρὸς βοῤῥάν

Beersheba, now Berossaba, as far as there is the border of Judaea to the south (seen) from Dan, near Paneas which borders (it) to the north

Eus.On. 50:1-12 and 166:20-21. Beersheba, now *Bīr as-Saba*ᶜ (coord. 130-072), is very often mentioned in the Bible and in other ancient literary sources. Some of the formulas used in the inscription are taken from *Eus.On.* 50:1ff., but combined in such a way that a somewhat strange kind of Greek emerged. Both Eusebius and the mosaicist are influenced by the Biblical formula 'from Dan to Beersheba' (e.g. Judg. 20:1; I Sam. 3:20; II Sam. 17:11 etc.) describing the totality of the promised land; they applied it to the political conditions in the Roman-Byzantine empire since Herodian times. Beersheba was the main military garrison of the so-called *limes Palaestinae* (the fortified border line of Palestine). Only this walled rectangular military encampment seems to be represented on the Madaba map. But this impression may be misleading: we note a colonnaded street in the east, a red-roofed ecclesiastical building in the west, and clustered houses in between – on the whole not typical for a military camp.

(100) ΑΡΑΔ˙ ΕΞ ΗϹ ΟΙ ΑΡΑΔΙΟΙ

Αραδ, ἐξ ἧς οἱ Αραδιοι

Arad, whence the Aradites

Eus.On. 14:1-3. The site of Biblical Arad (Numb. 33:40; Josh. 12:14; Judg. 1:16) is quite clear: it is *Tall ᶜArād* (coord. 162-076), about 32 km east of Beersheba and 27 km south of Hebron, well excavated in the sixties of our century. *Tall ᶜArād* seems to be meant by Eusebius. The remains of the Byzantine city have been found at *Ḫirbat Kusēfa* (coord. 156-073), some 6 km southwest of *Tall ᶜArād*, east of Beersheba. The mosaicist, however, represented Arad south of Beersheba in the southern desert, the reason for which is unknown. The 'Aradites' seem to originate from a Greek commentary on Gen. 10, the so-called 'Distribution of the Earth' (Διαμερισμὸς τῆς γῆς); the expression also occurs in the *Chronicon Paschale* (II,99).

(101) ΑϹΕΜΩΝΑ ΠΟΛΙϹ ΕΠΙ ΤΗϹ ΕΡΗ̣[ΜΟΥ] ΔΙΟΡΙΖΟΥϹΑ ΑΙΓΥ̣[ΠΤΟΝ] ΚΑΙ ΤΗΝ ΕΙϹ ΘΑΛ̣[ΑϹϹΑΝ] ΔΙ̣[ΕΞΟΔΟΝ]

Ασεμωνα πόλις ἐπὶ τῆς ἐρήμου διορίζουσα Αἴγυπτον καὶ τὴν εἰς θάλασσαν διέξοδον

Asemona (= Azmon), a city by the desert bordering Egypt and the going out of the Sea

Numb. 34:4f.; Josh. 15:4; *Eus.On.* 14:4-6. The text is almost literally quoted from Eusebius who paraphrased Numb. 34:5 according to the Greek Septuagint version. The place may be identical with *al-Qusēma*, 14 km northwest of *ᶜAyn Qudērāt* (= the Biblical Kadesh-Barnea), or with the plain called *al-Muwēliḥ* west of it.

(102) ΓΕΡΑΡΑ - ΓΕΡΑΡΑ˙ ΒΑϹΙΛΙΚΗ ΠΟΤΕ ΠΟΛΙϹ ΤΩΝ ΦΥΛΙϹΤΙΑΙΩΝ ΚΑΙ ΟΡΙΟΝ ΤΩΝ ΧΑΝΑΝΑΙΩΝ ΤΟ ΠΡΟϹ ΝΟΤΟΝ ΕΝΘΑ ΤΟ ΓΕΡΑΡΙΤΙΚΟΝ Ϲ̣Α̣ΛΤΟΝ

Γεραρα — Γεραρα, βασιλική ποτε πόλις τῶν Φυλιστιαίων καὶ ὅριον τῶν Χαναναίων τὸ πρὸς νότον ἔνθα τὸ Γεραριτικὸν σάλτον

Gerara (= Gerar) - Gerara, royal city of the Philistines and border of the Canaanites to the south where the *saltus Gerariticus* is

Gen. 20:1ff.; 26:1ff.; *Eus.On.* 60:7-14. The text is an excerpt from Eusebius (see above p. 23), supplemented by the political-administrative term *saltus Gerariticus* 'the domain of Gerar' which is often mentioned in Byzantine sources. The location is not quite clear: either *Tall aš-Šarīᶜa* (coord. 119-088) or, more probably, *Tall Abū Ḥurēra* (coord. 112-087), both of them about 20-25 km southeast of Gaza, apparently displaced on the Madaba map. By the way, Gerar did not belong to the Philistine city territories. The phrase 'royal city of the Philistines' is based upon Gen. 26:1 where king Abimelech of Gerar is made anachronistically a king of the Philistines.

(103) ΙΕΘΟΡ Η ΚΑΙ ΙΕΘΗΡΑ

Ιεθορ, ἡ καὶ Ιεθηρα

Jethor, also Jethera

Eus.On. 88:3ff. and 108:1-4. This is a very difficult and presumably unsolvable problem. Eusebius confused two villages: 1. Jattir (in Greek: Jether) in Judah, mentioned in Josh. 15:48 and undoubtedly identical with *Ḫirbat ᶜAttīr* (coord. 151-084), 6 km southeast of *aḏ-Ḏāharīya*; 2. Ether in Simeon (Josh. 19:7), whose name is most probably false, and whose site is unknown. The mosaicist took from Eusebius the name Jether, slightly changed, but he obviously did not mean the village in southern Judah, for he represented it southwest of Beersheba, perhaps on the road to Elusa. Did he mean the Simeonite Ether? That's more than doubtful, because a village of this name does not seem to have ever existed. Or did he know a village with a similar name and combined it wrongly with Eusebius and the Biblical reference?

(104) ΕΛΟΥϹΑ

Ελουσα

Elusa

Judith 1:9; not mentioned in *Eus.On.*, but so much the more in Christian, Jewish and Muslim sources, also on the Peutinger Plates. Elusa is identical with *al-Ḫalaṣa* (coord. 117-056), about 20 km southwest of Beersheba. It was founded by the Nabataeans in the 3rd century B.C. and became later on the capital of the Byzantine *Negeb* (*Palaestina Tertia*) and a bishop's see. The impressive ruins have been partly excavated after 1973 and 1980. The representation shows a middle-sized symbol with four towers and at least two red-roofed churches. Only one church, the Byzantine basilica, has been found up to now. The late Roman towers are not connected with a wall, but lean against the inside houses. It is, however, not likely that the mosaicist wanted to portray this peculiarity.

(105) ΦΩΤΙϹ

Φωτις

Photis

The village is identical with *Ḫirbat Fuṭēs* (coord. 114-081), about 7 km southwest of *Tall aš-Šarīᶜa*.

(106) ΟΡΔΑ

Ορδα

Orda

This form of the name is attested only here. Orda seems to have been for a time the capital of the *saltus Gerariticus* (nr. 102) and a bishop's see. Its location is doubtful: *Tall Ǧamma* (coord. 097-097), 12 km south of Gaza (Mazar) - more precisely: Roman-Byzantine remains directly south of the *Tall* - or *Ḫirbat* ^{c}*Irq*, about 10 km east-southeast of *Tall Ǧamma* (Alt)? See A. Alt, *Kleine Schriften 3* (1959) p. 382-391; B. Mazar, *PEQ 84* (1952) p. 48-51. If Orda is *Tall Ǧamma*, the village Jordan or Jardan, mentioned only by Fl. Josephus, *Jewish War* III:3:5 (§ 51), might be considered identical with it.

(107) ΚΛΗΡΟϹ ϹΥΜЄω[Ν]

Κλῆρος Συμεων

The lot of Simeon

For this expression see nr. 39.

(108) ωΓΑ

Ωγα

Oga

The village is mentioned only on the Madaba map. It is identical with *al-Hūǧ* (coord. 114-102), 14 km east of Gaza.

(109) [ΑϹ]ΑΛЄΑ

Ασαλεα

Asalea

Sozomenos, *hist. eccl.* III:14 (PG 67,1077). The village is identical with *an-Nazla* (coord. 100-104), about 4 km northeast of Gaza.

(110) [....]ωΝ

[...]ων

...on

Remains of a name which cannot be restored.

(111) ϹωΒΙΛΑ

Σωβιλα

Sobila

This village is attested only on the Madaba map. It is identical with *Ḫirbat az-Zubāla* (coord. 125-091), about 22 km west of *aḏ-Ḏāharīya* and 23 km south of *al-Falūǧa* (coord. 126-114).

(112) ΒЄΘΑΓΙΔЄΑ

Βεθαγιδεα

Bethagidea

This village, mentioned only on the Madaba map, is identical with *Ḫirbat al-Ǧundī* (coord. 113-092), 4 km north of *Tall Abū Ḥurēra* and 12 km southeast of Gaza.

(113) ЄΔΡΑΪΝ

Εδραϊν

Edrain

This village, attested only on the Madaba map, is identical with *Ḫirbat al-ᶜAdār* (coord. 096-093), about 7 km southwest of Gaza. The representation shows a walled town with a gate and three towers. Within the walls a brownish gable is visible, obviously not of a church.

(114) ΘΑΥΑΘΑ

Θαυαθα

Thauatha

Thauatha (or Tabatha) is identical with *Ḫirbat Umm at-Tūt*, about 2.5 km south of the mouth of *Wādī Ġazza* near *Šē ḫ Šubānī* (coord. 090-095). It is the birthplace of St. Hilarion (see nr. 121), the first monk in Palestine, whose life has been described by St. Jerome. The very small representation shows a fortress-like tower with a gate, portrayed in a perspective manner.

(115) CЄΑΝΑ

Σεανα

Seana

This village, attested only on the Madaba map, is identical with *Ḫirbat* (or *Tall*) *Siḥān* (coord. 105-095), 6 km southeast of Gaza.

(116) ΜΑΔЄΒΗΝΑ· Η ΝΥ̃ ΜΗΝΟΪC

Μαδεβηνα, ἡ νῦ(ν) Μηνοϊς

Madebena (= Madmena, Madmanna), now Menoïs

Josh. 15:31; *Eus.On.* 130:7-8. The mosaicist followed Eusebius who confused the village Madmanna in Judah (= *Ḫirbat Umm ad-Demina*, coord. 143-086, 4 km southwest of *aḏ-Ḏāharīya*) with Menoïs (= *Ḫirbat al-Māᶜīn*(coord. 093-077), about 10 km east-southeast of *Ḫān Yūnis*). Menoïs is mentioned in some Byzantine administrative texts.

(117) CYKOMAZωN

Συκομαζων

Sykomazon

This village, attested in Byzantine administrative texts and in the Jerusalem Targum, is identical with *Ḫirbat Sūq Māzin*, about 11 km southwest of Gaza. The simple representation shows a church inside the townlet.

(118) [Γ]ẠZA

Γαζα

Gaza

Ancient Gaza (now *Ġazza*) is very often mentioned in the Bible and in other literary sources from all periods of history. The city was the most important political and commercial centre on the southern Palestinian coast. Its large representation, approximately half of which is preserved, cannot be easily explained, mainly because only small tentative excavations have been made there and because Byzantine Gaza is covered by the still inhabited Old City, situated upon a huge *Tall*. The city is walled. We note five towers, two of them flanking the southern gate. The ground plan is of roughly circular or elliptic shape like the *Tall* within the ancient city wall, very similar to the representation of Jerusalem. Two colonnaded streets (*cardo maximus* and *decumanus*) are shown. The main street runs from the eastern gate (formerly *Bāb al-Ḫalīl*) to the western gate (formerly *Bāb Maimās*), its course is approximately identical with present *as-Sūq al-kabīr*. The other street goes from the southern gate (formerly *Bāb ad-Dārūn*) to a square in the very centre of the city, situated in the area of present *Ḫān az-Zēt* and its environs. Obviously, there is no intersection, as in the modern city: the street coming from *Bāb ad-Dārūn* does not lead to *Bāb ᶜAsqalān*, the northern gate, but disappears in the medley of lanes around the centre. Directly inside the eastern gate we see another square place with some kind of passage-way to the north, and leading to a large semicircular building surrounded by colonnades on its southern side, most likely a theatre, whose stage even has the conventional three gates. If we follow the main street to the west, we see on the south side a small domed building, probably a public fountain (Nymphaion), and opposite to it a small square. Another small square is seen on the north side of the main street beyond the central square, or is it the beginning of a street leading to a northern gate (the present street passing *Ḫān al-Kittān* or *Sūq al-Ḥağar*)? In the southwestern quarter we note two churches: a larger one on the left with a portico, and a smaller one on the right. The larger one is probably the main basilica of Gaza, built by the empress Eudocia around 440 above the ruins of the temple of Zeus Marnas (Marnas = our Lord), the so-called Cretian Zeus, in Greek also named ὁ πάτριος θεός. The smaller church might have been devoted to St. Stephanus or St. Sergius. There is, however, a problem concerning the main basilica. According to the principle of inheritance of sanctuaries we may assume that the basilica was situated on the same place as the present *Ǧāmiᶜ al-kabīr* 'the Great Mosque', the successor of the Crusaders' church of St. John. But *Ǧāmiᶜ al-kabīr* is not located southwest, but northeast of the central square. Is what we think to be the main basilica another church, while the main basilica was in the broken northeastern part of the city?

(119) [ΜΑΙΟΥΜΑϹ Η] ΚΑΙ ΝΕΑ[ΠΟ]ΛΙϹ

Μαιουμας ἡ καὶ Νεάπολις

Maiumas, also Neapolis

This is the seaport of ancient Gaza, attested as an independent city in several Byzantine sources. It is identical with *al-Mīna* (coord. 096-103), more precisely: with the ruins south of the road which runs from ancient Gaza to the Sea, about 4 km west of the Old City of Gaza. For the name Maiumas see nr. 12. The bishops of Gaza first resided at Maiumas, because Gaza itself was an obstinate pagan city and offered resistance to christianity. The fragmentarily preserved representation shows a remarkable city. We see the eastern gate flanked by towers, a street leading to the west and another one branching off to the north, finally at least three red-roofed churches.

(120) ΤΟ ΤȢ ΑΓΙȢ ΒΙΚΤΟΡΟϹ

Τὸ τοῦ ἁγίου Βικτορος

(The sanctuary) of St. Victor

The Piacenza pilgrim (ch. 33) describes the burial place of St. Victor as situated inside Maiumas-Neapolis. The mosaicist, however, represented the nice little memorial building with a red-roofed portico outside the city, between Maiumas and ancient Gaza.

(121) ΤΟ [ΤΟΥ ΑΓΙΟΥ] Ι[ΛΑΡΙΩΝΟϹ]

Τὸ τοῦ ἁγίου Ιλαριωνος

(The sanctuary) of St. Hilarion

This memorial place was situated in or near *Dēr al-Balaḥ* (coord. 089-092), about 10 km southwest of Gaza (H. Donner, *ZDPV 83, 1967, p. 28f.*). St. Hilarion of Gaza (291-361 [?]) was born in Thauatha (nr. 114). He was one of the fathers and founders of Palestinian monasticism and died on Cyprus. His life has been described by St. Jerome. His tomb, also mentioned in several Christian sources, was located within a monastery. No traces of this inscription can be seen on the drawing.

The following sites (nrs. 122-129) are situated along the most important coastal road connecting Palestine with Egypt, the so-called *via maris* (Way of the Sea).

(122) ΡΑΦ[ΙΑ]
Ραφια
Raphia

Raphia was the boundary town between Palestine and Egypt. The mosaicist seems to have associated inland Raphia (= *Ḫirbat Bīr Rafaḥ*, 2.5 km northwest of present *Rafaḥ*, coord. 077-077) and Raphia by the sea (= *Tall Rafaḥ* on the sea shore, coord. 075-076).

(123) Β[ΗΤ]ΥΛΙΟΝ
Βητυλιον
Betylion

The ancient names of this village vary slightly (Bitylion, Bitolion, Betulia, Bethelia). It is identical with one of the ruins near *Kurūm aš-Šēḫ*, 15 km southwest of *Rafaḥ* as the crow flies: either *Tall Ǧanīn*, or *Tall Abū Salīma*, or – most likely – *Tall aš-Šēḫ* Zuwayid (A. Alt, *ZDPV 49, 1926, p. 236-242.333ff.; RB 48, 1939, p. 227f.544-547; RB 49, 1940, p. 224-227*). We note the red roof of a church. The village has often been confused with Bethelia, the home town of the famous historian Sozomenos (*hist. eccl.* V:15; VII:28.32; VIII:14), situated not very far from *Bēt Laḥyā* northeast of Gaza. A pagan temple was there, erected on the top of a hill, transformed into a church by the monk Hilarion in the early 4th century. Did the mosaicist fall a victim of this confusion as well?

(124) ΟΡΟΙ ΑΙΓΥΠΤȣ Κ϶ ΠΑΛΑΙCΤΙΝΗC
Ὅροι Αἰγύπτου κ(αὶ) Παλαιστίνης
The border between Egypt and Palestine

Eus.On. 50:18-20 locates the border near the village Bethaphu.

(125) ΡΙΝΟΚΟΡΟΥΡΑ
Ρινοκορουρα
Rhinokorura

Rhinokorura (also Rhinokolura) is often mentioned in classical, Byzantine and later sources (e.g. Fl. Josephus, *Jewish War* I:14:2 [§ 277]; IV:11:5 [§ 662]; *Antiquities* XIII:15:4; XIV:14:2), also on the Peutinger Plates. It was situated near modern *al-ᶜArīš* at the mouth of *Wādī 'l-ᶜArīš*. We see the red roofs of two churches. It is very interesting that, according to *Abū Ṣāliḥ*, the ruins of two churches were still visible in the Middle Ages. Rhinokorura was a bishop's see since the 4th century. There is a remarkable local tradition: it was here that Noah bequeathed the heritage to his three sons Shem, Ham and Japheth. One of the churches might have been devoted to St. Noah.

126 ΟϹΤΡΑΚΙΝΗ

Οστρακινη

Ostrakine

This village, represented as a basilica flanked by two towers, is identical with *Ḫirbat al-Fulūsīya*. It was a bishop's see since the 4th century. Local Christian traditions are attested concerning the prophet Habakkuk and the Apostles Simon Judas, Thaddaeus and Jacob son of Alphaeus.

127 ΤΟ ΚΑϹΙΝ

Τὸ Κασιν

Kasin (= Kasion, Kasios, Casius)

This is a settlement near the sanctuary of Zeus Kasios, the Hellenistic-Roman successor of an ancient Baal Zaphon. The village, often mentioned in Byzantine sources, was situated at the western edge of the *Ṣabḫāt al-Bardawīl*, the ancient Sirbonic Lake, about 15 km east of Pelusium (nr. 134).

128 ΤΟ ΠΕΝΤΑϹΧΟ[Ι]ΝΟΝ

Τὸ Πενταςχοινον

Pentaschoinon

The village is probably identical with *Maḥammadīya*, not far from Kasi(o)n (nr. 127). Roman remains have been found there, but nothing from Christian times, except two cemeteries.

129 ΤΟ Α[ΦΝΑΙΟΝ]

Τὸ Αφναιον

Aphnaion

The village Aphnaion (less frequently called Aphthaion, see e.g. Georgios Cyprios 695) was a bishop's see since 431 at the latest. Its location is not quite clear: ruins about 1.5 km west of *Maḥammadīya* (J. Clédat) or *Qaṭya* (F.-M. Abel)?

Excursus: Lower Egypt

The geographical features have been explained above p. 68f. Additional peculiarities, however, must be discussed here. The representation of Lower Egypt differs in more than one respect from that of other sections of the Madaba map – a fact to which scholars usually do not pay attention. A clear description of the differences will be the first step to a pertinent interpretation of this neglected part of the mosaic map.

1. On the whole, the Madaba map is an illustration of God's salvation history according to the Holy Bible. But strangely enough, the representation of Lower Egypt does not correspond with this principle. We may recognize it by the *desiderata*, that is by the lack of important Biblical facts and themes which should be expected on the map. Let us consider some examples. The story of Joseph and his brothers (Gen. 37.39-50) is missing: that story according to which Joseph settled his father's family in the land of Goshen in the eastern Delta, especially in the *Wādī aṭ-Ṭumēlāt*. Nothing is reported of Israel's stay in Egypt (Exod. 1-12), of their oppression and of their building the store cities of Pithom and Ramses (Exod. 1:11), of the glorious Exodus from Egypt (Exod. 13-15). The figure of Moses is completely absent, and the crossing of the Sea of Reeds is not mentioned – the latter, probably, because Byzantine tradition located this event at the northernmost point of the Gulf of Suez beyond the preserved parts of the map. Furthermore, we find no trace either of the prophet Jeremiah's stay in Egypt (Jerem. 42-44) or of the flight of the Holy Family to Egypt (Matth. 2) where they were thought to have reached Heliopolis or even Memphis. Inscriptions in the style of the Madaba map referring to such Biblical themes can easily be invented, e.g. Τάνις, ἐκ ταύτης ἦν ὁ ἅγιος Μωϋσῆς 'Tanis, whence was St. Moses', or Γεσεμ, ἐν ᾗ κατῴκησεν Ιακωβ ἅμα τοῖς υἱοῖς αὐτοῦ 'Goshen, where Jacob dwelt together with his sons' (according to *Eus.On.* 62:10f.) etc. Such proposals tend to do the work of the mosaicist for him. The question arises: why did he omit his duty?

2. The main literary source of the Madaba map was Eusebius *Onomasticon of Biblical Place Names*, as described above (see p. 22-24). The mosaicist used it exhaustively, except in preparing the representation of Lower Egypt. Eusebius mentions 10 or 11 cities and villages in the Delta, the mosaicist 14 – but only two of them are attested in Eusebius'

Onomasticon as well as on the mosaic of Madaba, namely Sais (nr. 141) and Tanis (nr. 138). The same is true of other suggested sources of the map (see above p. 24-25). We get the strange impression that the mosaicist used a small library of important books until he began to prepare the mosaic of Lower Egypt, then he closed the door of this library and disregarded it. Why did he do so, and what sources did he really use for the Delta of the Nile?

3. The Madaba map is the most exact example of ancient cartography before the beginning of modern cartography in the 19th century. Its few errors (see above p. 18-20) do not alter its value. In the relatively small section of Lower Egypt, however, the accumulation of inaccuracies is striking. The sites of the cities of Xois (nr. 142) and Sais (nr. 141) have changed: Xois was situated near modern *Saḫā*, about 24 km southeast of *Tall Faraᶜūn*, i.e. east of the Sebennitic arm; and Sais was situated near *Kafr az-Zayāt* north of *Ṣā al-Ḥagar* at the arm of Rosette, i.e. west of the Sebennitic arm. Consequently, the Saitic arm is misrepresented on the map. It does not branch off to the right (east), but to the left (west) when seen from the Sebennitic arm. The village Henikiu (nr. 135) is most probably identical with *Kōm Razīn*, about 9 km southwest of *Manūf* and east of the Canopic arm in the so-called Prosopitic district. On the map it is too far to the east. Pelusium (nr. 134) was mainly on the east side of the Pelusiac arm, on the Madaba map we find it on the west side. Other mistakes have been discussed and explained above. Did the mosaicist ever see Lower Egypt, did he visit the Nile Delta?

As to his sources we mentioned Herodotus, *hist.* II:17:3-6 (see above p. 67-68). But what principles did the mosaicist use to choose the cities and villages to be represented on his map? Obviously neither Biblical tradition nor pilgrims' requirements were used. Did he want to portray the Christian Lower Egypt in Byzantine times by giving the ecclesiastical centres and bishops' residences? If this be the case, we should compare the Madaba map with the lists of Byzantine bishoprics, e.g. with the *Descriptio Orbis Romani*, written by Georgius Cyprius in the reign of the emperor Phokas (602-610). The *Descriptio* mentions 50 metropolitan cities in Lower Egypt, the Madaba map 14 only, five of which are absent from the *Descriptio* while very significant bishops' sees are lacking on the Madaba map: e.g. Bubastis, Leontopolis, Naucratis, Taua, Cleopatris, Busiris etc. In a word: this is certainly no representation of ecclesiastical Lower Egypt in the 6th century.

Consequently, we should examine the relation of the represented cities and villages to the road system in the Nile Delta. There were three main roads, running approximately along the collateral lines of the Delta triangle. We know these roads from written itineraries, collected for instance in the so-called *Itinerarium Antonini*, and from the famous Peutinger Plates. The first main road ran from Pelusium to Memphis, the second from Alexandria to Memphis, the third from Pelusium to Alexandria. No one will be surprised to hear that all cities and villages shown on the Madaba map are situated on one of these main roads, except Thennesos. Thennesos (nr. 140), known from Byzantine and early Arab sources, was a commercial town and a seaport upon a small island within the lagoon region of *Birkat* (also *Baḥr*) *Manzāla*, nowadays *Tall* (also *Kōm*) *Tinnis*. This town, of course, was connected with the inland: there must have been roads, although we do not know them precisely, probably to *Heracleopolis parva* (nr. 137), or to Tanis (nr. 138), or to both of them. The strange rhombus near Thennesos seems to be a hint of the lagoon area in the northwestern part of the Delta – but this assumption is far from being certain.

To sum up, the mosaicist used the classical description of the Delta, written by Herodotus, and a profane Roman-Byzantine itinerary, the latter not necessarily identical with what we read in the *Itinerarium Antonini*, but similar to it. We cannot exclude his also using a Roman-Byzantine road map. However, it seems better to assume that he did not, since the inaccuracies in locating the places and minor arms of the Nile are quite intelligible, when he did not use a map which could have corrected him. It was sufficient to know where the big cities of Pelusium, Alexandria and Memphis were situated: after that the mosaicist could complete the representation according to his itinerary.

Finally, another problem must be mentioned here. Some of the cities in Lower Egypt are represented with very peculiar symbols: Pelusium (nr. 134), Henikiu (nr. 135), Athribis (nr. 136), Sethroïtes (nr. 137), Tanis (nr. 138), and Thmuis (nr. 139). These symbols show buildings and major streets in a seemingly exact manner, but in quite another style compared to Palestinian cities. We do not know why. Although the mosaicist was not familiar with Lower Egypt, he portrayed these cities as if he were very familiar with them. Did he use sources containing local traditions about Saints, martyrs and bishops, such as those we know of from Greek and Coptic sources? The question remains unanswered.

(130) ΠΗΛΟΥC[ΙΑΚΟΝ]

Πηλουσιακὸν (στόμα)

The Pelusiac arm

See above p. 68.

(131) CAÏ[TIKON]

Σαϊτικὸν (στόμα)

The Saitic arm

See above p. 68.

(132) CЄBЄNNY[TIKON]

Σεβεννυτικὸν (στόμα)

The Sebennitic arm

See above p. 68.

(133) BOΛBYTIKO[N]

Βολβυτικὸν (στόμα)

The Bolbytic (also Bulbytic) arm

See above p. 68.

(134) ṬO ΠΗΛΟΥCIN

Τὸ Πηλουσιν

Pelusin (= Pelusion, Pelusium)

The city of Pelusium is identical with *Tall al-Faramā*, situated on the east (not on the west) bank of the ancient Pelusiac arm. This most important city, often mentioned by classical, Byzantine and Muslim authors, was especially famous for its flourishing textile industry (the English word blouse, borrowed from French, is derived from Pelusium!). It was a bishop's see since the 4th century at the latest, and the home or place of martyrdom of many Saints, monks and martyrs, such as Antonius, Apa Anoua, Apatil, Isidor of Pelusium (360-435?) etc. There were monasteries in the vicinity of the city, not represented on the Madaba map. One of the most common Christian traditions refers to the Holy Family which is said to have made a halt in Pelusium on its flight to Egypt (Matth. 2) - quite intelligible, because Pelusium was the door to Egypt for people coming from Asia. Unfortunately, it is very difficult and nearly hopeless to compare the large representation on the Madaba map with the remains on *Tall al-Faramā*. Only some smaller surveys and soundings have been made there (J. Flinders Petrie, J. Clédat). Petty remains of a temple of Zeus Casius (see nr. 127) were found, but no traces of Christian churches at all. On the mosaic map we see about the half of a large walled city with three preserved towers and two gates close to each other in the northern part of the wall (below). Strange to say, no street runs southward from these gates. Three colonnaded streets go from west to east, one of them adjacent to the northern wall. Three churches with red roofs are visible: the largest one near the southern wall, another one in the southwest, and a very small one in the southern quarter of the city. Houses are clustered in between, one of them with a yellowish-golden triangular pediment (?), but without a red roof. This fragmentarily preserved representation remains a mystery.

(135) Η ΝΙΚΙΟΥ

'Η Νικίου

Henikiu (= Of Nikios)

This village, often mentioned by classical, Byzantine and Muslim authors and noted on the Peutinger Plates, is most probably identical with *Kōm Razīn*, some 9 km southwest of *Manūf* and about 25 km from *Ibšādī* (which is situated near ancient Arsinoë/Cleopatris). Henikiu was the capital of the Prosopitic district; on the Madaba map it is much too far to the east. It was a bishop's see since the 4th century at the latest. We know some of its martyrs from Coptic sources, such as Sarapam(m)on, Isaac of Difray, Makarios of Antiochia, Theodoros Stratelates etc. The Holy Family is said to have rested there for seven days, in the course of which little Jesus healed a demoniac. Arab and Ethiopian sources mention many churches, destroyed by the Persians in the 6th century. The representation looks like a rectangular walled monastery: one main gate and four towers are visible, two of them with smaller gates. Inside the wall we note two red-roofed churches with porticos, or are they cloister arches? The latter could be suggested by the columns being not only in front of the churches but seemingly also around them. The remains of two churches dedicated to St. Sarapam(m)on have been indicated archaeologically – are they identical with the two churches on the Madaba map?

(136) ΑΘΡΙΒΙϹ

Αθριβις

Athribis

The city is identical with *Tall Atrīb* near *Banhā al-ᶜAsal*. The representation shows a walled city with two towers and a red-roofed basilica apparently built upon and into the wall with an upper and a lower gate entrance. Behind the basilica we see a colonnaded street running from north to south. Athribis was one of the most important and most frequented cities of Lower Egypt, and a bishop's see since the 4th century at the latest. It is often mentioned by classical, Byzantine and Arab authors, also on the Peutinger Plates. Coptic sources tell us of several martyrs, such as Didymus, Apa Anoup, Sergius nephew of the governor Cyprianus etc. In the Middle Ages, and perhaps earlier, there was a monastery (according to others: a church) of the Virgin St. Mary who had worked miracles there. The Tetrapylon, mentioned by Coptic authors and indicated archaeologically, is not represented on the Madaba map.

137 ϹЄΘΡΟΪΤΗϹ

Σεθροϊτης

Sethroïtes (= *Heracleopolis parva*)

The city of *Heracleopolis parva* was later referred to by the name of the district Sethroïs in which it was situated. It is identical with *Tall Balīm* (also called *Tall aš-Šarīg*). It was a bishop's see since the 4th century. Christian authors tell of a monastery near (but not in) Heracleopolis. The somewhat strange representation looks like a single red-roofed church, erected on the top of a hill, with an annex and no less than three gate entrances. The rectangular object on the left side remains unexplained.

138 ΤΑΝΙϹ

Τανις

Tanis

The city is identical with *Ṣān al-Ḥagar*. The small representation shows an irregular wall with two very high towers, apparently without any churches. A third lower tower is seen on the left, as are two gates leading into the city. The picture looks like one of those medieval cities in Italy, whose inhabitants dwelt in high towers, e.g. Florence, Siena, or San Gimignano. Tanis was a bishop's see since the 4th century at the latest, and a focus for many Biblical traditions concerning Egypt, although none are indicated on the Madaba map. Or could the rhombus between Tanis and Thennesos (nr. 140) be the 'field of Zoan' (= Tanis) mentioned in Ps. 78:12?

139 ΘΜΟΥΪϹ

Θμουϊς

Thmuis

Thmuis, very similar to Tanis (nr. 138), is identical with *Tall Timay al-Amīd*. It is often mentioned in Byzantine and later sources. It was a bishop's see since the first half of the 3rd century and the place where St. Phileas was martyred in 306. We note two towerlike buildings with red roofs, and two gate entrances.

140 ΘЄΝΝΗϹΟϹ

Θεννησος

Thennesos

A commercial town and a seaport, identical with *Tall* (also *Kōm*) *Tinnis*, situated upon a small island in the *Birkat* (or *Baḥr*) *Manzāla*, often mentioned in Greek and Arab sources. It was a bishop's see since the 5th century. The representation is almost completely lost. Is the rhombus above the inscription a hint of the lagoon region in which the city was situated? Or an indication of the 'field of Zoan' in Ps. 78:12 (see nr. 138)?

(141) CAÏC

Σαΐς

Sais

The city of Sais, a bishop's see since the 4th century, was situated near *Kafr az-Zayāt*, north of *Ṣā al-Ḥagar*. It is displaced on the Madaba map (see above p. 80). The simple representation is almost completely lost.

(142) ΞΟΪC

Ξοΐς

Xois

The city of Xois, a bishop's see since the 4th century, was situated near modern *Saḫā* in the district of *Kafr aš-Šēḫ*, about 24 km southeast of *Tall al-Faraᶜūn* (= the ancient Buto). It is displaced on the Madaba map (see above p. 80). The simple representation shows three towers and one gate.

(143) Η ΠΑΥΛΙΝΟΥ

Ἡ Παυλίνου

Hepaulinu (= Of Paulinos)

A totally unknown village, attested in no known literary source.

(144) ЄΡΜȢΠΟΛΙC

Ἑρμούπολις

Hermupolis (= *Hermopolis parva*)

The city of Hermupolis is identical with modern *Damanhūr* (*al-Waḥš*). It is often mentioned by classical, Byzantine and Arab authors, also on the Peutinger Plates. It was for some time the capital of the hinterland of Alexandria and a bishop's see since the 4th century. The simple representation shows three towers, one gate entrance, no churches.

(145) ΧΟΡΤΑCω

Χορτασω

Chortaso

The village is identical with *Qarṭasā* north of *Damanhūr*. It was christianized in the 4th century at the latest, but never was a bishop's see. Greek and Coptic sources mention the martyrdom of St. Habakkuk and St. Šenūfe (around 306). The simple representation, however, shows no churches.

(146) ΚΑΙΝȣΠΟΛ

Καινούπολ<ις>

Kainupolis

An unknown city or village.

(147) Η ΧΑ̣[ΙΡЄΟΥ]

Ἡ Χαιρέου

Hechaireu (= Of Chaireos)

This village, often mentioned by Byzantine and Muslim authors, is identical with ruins near *al-Karyūn* (perhaps *Kōm al-Gīza*?). Christians and Christian churches are not attested in literary sources earlier than the Middle Ages. The simple representation is almost completely lost.

Section D: Jerusalem

Above the representation of the Holy City we read the following inscription in big red letters:

Η ΑΓΙΑ ΠΟΛΙϹ ΙΈΡΟΥϹΑ[ΛΗΜ]
Ἡ ἁγία πόλις Ιερουσαλημ
The Holy City of Jerusalem

Undoubtedly, the picture of Jerusalem is the most impressive image on the whole Madaba map. It is much larger than that of any other city in Palestine or Lower Egypt. The reason is clear: Jerusalem was considered 'the navel of the earth', the very centre of God's salvation history, the place of Jesus Christ's death and resurrection. We see a walled city elliptic in shape, protected by 19 towers, seen from a viewpoint high up in the west and outlined in some kind of perspective. Consequently, the western part of the city-wall is shown from outside, the eastern part from inside. The mosaicist, however, used the perspective outline generally, except for some important features inside the city, as he sought to portray Jerusalem and its buildings as precisely as possible. Therefore he opened up the colonnades of the main street running from north to south, turning the western colonnade upside down. Nearly all buildings inside the wall face the spectator, except the Church of the Anastasis (7), an ecclesiastical building south of it (8), and the Church of the House of Caiphas (16). The column standing on the oval square south of the Damascus Gate (1) is seen from the south, as is the arch leading to the secondary street going from north to south in the eastern part of the city.

The Madaba map shows Jerusalem as it was in the middle of the 6th century A.D., 14 centuries ago. But strange to say, the main lines of the city plan have been preserved up to our times, approximately and with respect to some peculiarities. Visitors are advised to climb the tower of the Lutheran Redeemer's Church, near the so-called *Mūristān* not far from the Church of Holy Sepulchre. This is the very best place to look at the Old City from above – and lo, it is the city represented on the Madaba map! There is only one main exception. The Turkish wall, built after 1517 by the Sultan *Sulēmān the Magnificent*, runs from *Bāb al-Muġāriba* (4) to *Bāb an-Nabī Dā'ūd* (5), leaving outside the southwest hill (the so-called Christian Sion) and the southeast hill down to the pool of Siloam. On the

Madaba map these hills are inside the city-wall where the Byzantine empress Eudocia enclosed them around 440 A.D. when she extended the wall to the south.

Fortunately, there are two literary descriptions of Jerusalem which are roughly contemporary with the Madaba map: the so-called 'Short Account of Jerusalem' (*Breviarius de Hierosolyma*) from about 550 and the report of an anonymous pilgrim coming from Piacenza who visited Palestine shortly after 570. Translations and explanations of these Latin texts are given by J. Wilkinson, *Jerusalem Pilgrims before the Crusades* (1977) p. 59-61.79-89, and by H. Donner, *Pilgerfahrt ins Heilige Land. Die ältesten Berichte christlicher Palästinapilger* (1979), p. 226-239.240-314. The representation of Jerusalem on the Madaba map may be interpreted as a pictorial comment on these literary sources, although the mosaicist certainly did not know them. In any case, this coincidence is a stroke of luck. There are suggestions for the identification of nearly all ecclesiastical and profane buildings inside the city (see the selected bibliography on p. 99f.). Some are certain, some probable and others doubtful. In the present booklet we shall confine ourselves to identifications which are undoubtedly true or most probable; we do not want to interfere with the scholarly discussion. Therefore only selected items are explained, such as the city gates (1-6), churches and monasteries with red roofs (7-18), and some other buildings (19-25).

The gates of Byzantine Jerusalem, still exactly or approximately on the same spots today, are described in a clockwise direction, beginning with the

1 Damascus Gate, called St. Stephen's Gate in the 6th century, now *Bāb al-^{c}Amūd*. It is flanked by two towers and leads to an oval square containing a single column. This column, the source of the gate's Arabic name, was apparently erected in honour of a Roman or Byzantine emperor and may have carried his statue. It is mentioned by the bishop Arculf around 680 (I, ch. XI). The famous Neapolis road, starting from the Damascus Gate to the north, is partly represented in white cubes. St. Stephen's basilica north of the gate, built around 444 by the empress Eudocia and destroyed in 614 by the Persians, is not shown on the map.

2 St. Stephen's Gate, called Gate of the Sheep Pool (see nr. 10) in the 6th century, now *Bāb Sittī Maryam*.

3 Golden Gate or Gate Beautiful (see Acts 3:2), leading to the temple area, now *Bāb ar-Raḥma*, also *Bāb et-Tauba*.

4 Dung Gate, now *Bāb al-Muġāriba*.

5 Sion Gate, now *Bāb an-Nabī Dā'ūd*, was originally situated more to the east. It is the goal of the main street which comes from Damascus Gate.

6 Jaffa Gate, called Gate of the Tower (*porta Purgu*, Theodosius ch. 3) in the 6th century, now *Bāb al-Ḫalīl*.

Gates 4 and 5 no longer lead outside the city because of the empress Eudocia's new wall which enclosed the southern hills of Jerusalem. Five streets are shown, each represented in white and brownish cubes similar to those of the oval square inside the Damascus Gate. The main colonnaded street – the *Cardo Maximus* of Roman-Byzantine Jerusalem – runs from the Damascus Gate to the Sion Gate: its western colonnade is interrupted by the staircase of the Anastasis-Church (7), the eastern one ends in front of the Nea Theotokos-Church (12). This street line is still preserved today. It is approximately identical with (from north to south) *Ṭarīq Bāb al-ᶜAmūd*, *Sūq al-ᶜAṭṭārīn* (market of the spice-dealers), the threefold row of *Sūq al-Laḥḥāmīn*, *Sūq aṣ-Ṣuyyāġ* (market of the goldsmiths) and *Sūq al-Ḫowāǧāt* (market of the tradespeople), finally *Ṭarīq Bāb an-Nabī Dā'ūd* (also called *Sūq al-Ḥusūr*). The street line does not reach *Bāb an-Nabī Dā'ūd* (5) which has been displaced about 100 m to the west. A second street begins on the east side of the oval square under an arch and runs to the south until the Dung Gate (4). It is colonnaded as well, but only the eastern colonnade is visible. This street follows the line of what was called Tyropoion Valley (valley of the cheesemakers) and is identical with modern *Ṭarīq al-Wād* which no longer leads to the Dung Gate but ends beforehand in the latitude of *Bāb as-Silsila*. The third street, running from St. Stephen's Gate (2) to the *Ṭarīq al-Wād*, is the beginning of the Christian *Via Dolorosa*, at present called *Ṭarīq Bāb Sittī Maryam* or *Ṭarīq al-Ḥabs*. A fourth street without columns – the *Decumanus* of Roman-Byzantine Jerusalem – starts from Jaffa Gate (6) and runs to the east. It seems to end at the main street (*Cardo Maximus*). This is, however, an error: the street crossed the main street and led to the Herodian wall of the Holy Area (at the present *Bāb as-Silsila*). This continuation presented difficulties to the mosaicist: he confined himself to indicate the so-called Tetrapylon at the crossing of both streets by two columns which he represented within the wall of a church east of the main street (18). The *Decumanus* is roughly identical with Christian King David Street, also called

Sūq al-Bazār or formerly *Sūq al-Bidār* (cornmarket), and its continuation *Ṭarīq Bāb as-Silsila* (formerly called *Ṭarīq as-Saray al-Qadīm*). The fifth street, finally, branches off the *Decumanus* to the south: this is, probably, the Armenian Street (*Ḥārat al-Arman*). On the whole, we have to recognize the astonishing fact that the street network of Byzantine Jerusalem remains essentially unchanged today, even in the modern Jewish quarter in the southern part of the Old City.

Let us continue with the main churches of Byzantine Jerusalem, as far as they are represented on the Madaba map:

7 Church of the Anastasis (Resurrection), also called Holy Sepulchre. It is a complex of buildings between the main street and the Holy Sepulchre itself, erected by the emperor Constantine between 326 and 336; its interior was renewed by Justinian in the middle of the 6th century, then destroyed by the Persians in 614. The very best description of this complex is given by Eusebius, *Vita Constantini* III:25-40. We learn from Eusebius that the whole complex consisted of five parts (from east to west): a) a staircase leading up from the main street to the outer wall pierced by three gates; b) the exterior court with columns; c) the basilica with five naves, called Martyrium; d) the inner courtyard with Golgotha in its southeastern corner, situated under the open sky; e) the dome over the Tomb of the Lord, called Rotunda of the Anastasis. This monumental complex, orientated to the west, was about 150 m long and 75 m wide. It is mentioned, of course, by all pilgrims and by nearly all Christian authors as the most important sanctuary of Christianity. The representation on the Madaba map is the only existing picture of it. To show every detail and the orientation to the west, the mosaicist reversed its image contradicting the principles of perspective, representing the staircase on the top and the dome at the bottom. Moreover, he seems to have simplified a little bit. The outer court is missing, the four steps seem to lead directly to the façade of the Martyrium. Or did he mean the three gates of the outer court, whilst the façade of the basilica – according to recent excavations – had five gates? If this be the case, the white cubes in the 'upper' part of what seems to be the façade might be an indication of the outer court, and the brownish cubes in the 'lower' part might belong to the façade itself. The Martyrium with a yellow triangular pediment and a red sloping roof is clearly depicted. Between the Martyrium and the dome of the Resurrection we see five or six black cubes, indicating either the courtyard 'before the Cross' (note one black cube right above the row!) or the Lord's Tomb itself. The dimensions of this representation show and underline the importance of this greatest of Christian sanctuaries.

8 Baptistery of the Church of the Anastasis (?). This building with a flat red roof, two small doors and one window, is reversed as is the Church of the Anastasis. It stands west of a light-brown trapezoidal space, probably the market-place (*Forum*) of Roman-Byzantine Jerusalem. Its identification with the baptistery of the Holy Sepulchre is uncertain, since the only extant reference to any kind of baptistery is by the anonymous pilgrim of Bordeaux (*Itinerarium Burdigalense* 17): 'at the back there is a bath in which children are baptized'.

9 An unknown church, considered by some scholars to be the Monastery of St. Serapion, mentioned in the so-called *List of the Slain*, but this identification cannot be proven. The church was situated not far from the Damascus Gate (1).

10 Church of the Sheep Pool (*Probatica*), built in the first half of the 5th century over the Sheep Pool of Bethesda (John 5:1-16) where Jesus healed a paralysed man, was destroyed by the Persians in 614. The church is first mentioned by Peter the Iberian (Raabe, p. 94) and later by other Christian pilgrims and Early Fathers. It is interesting to see that the church was associated from the very beginning with St. Mary, the Lord's mother, commemorating her birth. In the Middle Ages this tradition passed to the nearby church of St. Anne. The façade of the church of St. Mary at Bethesda faces southward, for reasons of perspective. The remains of the church have been excavated by the French White Fathers.

11 Church on the Pinnacle of the Temple (*Pinna Templi*), commemorating how Jesus Christ was tempted by the Satan who said: 'Throw yourself down!' (Matth. 4:5f.; Luke 4:9-12). This church was situated in the southeastern corner of the temple esplanade (*Ḥaram aš-Šarīf*). It is attested only on the Madaba map and in the *Breviarius de Hierosolyma*: 'From there you come to the Pinnacle of the Temple on which Satan tempted our Lord Jesus Christ. A cross-shaped basilica is there.'

12 New Church of the Mother of God (*Nea Theotokos*), built by the emperor Justinian and consecrated on November 20, 542 - a fact important for dating the Madaba map (see above p. 14). This new church (for the old one, cf. nr. 10) is thoroughly described by Procopius of Caesarea, *De aedificiis* V:6 and mentioned by several Christian pilgrims and authors. It was situated in the present Jewish quarter of the Old City between Dung Gate and Sion Gate. Remains were recently discovered by excavations: the apse being inside, a corner being outside the Turkish wall. On the Madaba map we see a large basilica with a double yellow

portal, accessible from the main street not far from Sion Gate (5). To the left of the church, behind the eastern colonnade of the main street, there is a gateway leading outside the inner wall. This gate, otherwise unknown, lies between the Sion Gate (5) and the Dung Gate (4), or is it the entrance to the 'guest house for men and women' belonging to the church and mentioned by the Piacenza pilgrim (ch. 23)?

13 Church north of the Pool of Siloam, commemorating how Jesus Christ healed a man born blind (John 9:1-6). The church was built either under the emperor Valentinian (364-375) or, more probably, by the empress Eudocia before 450. It is first mentioned by Peter the Iberian (Raabe, p. 56) and described by the Piacenza pilgrim (ch. 24). The building south of the fragmentarily preserved basilica was believed to have been erected over the Pool of Siloam itself, serving as a bath. This is, however, quite uncertain, because the pool seems to have been situated under the open sky.

14 Basilica on Mount Sion, one of the most important churches in Jerusalem, second only to that of the Holy Sepulchre. It was built on the Christian Sion (the southwestern hill) around 340 as successor to an older Church of the Apostles thought to be the house of the Apostles (Acts 12: 12). The archdeacon Theodosius (ch. 7) called it the 'mother of all churches' (*mater omnium ecclesiarum*), obviously because of the story of Pentecost (Acts 2:1-4). The representation shows a very large basilica with a big double yellow portal. North of it we see a construction of brownish cubes with two yellow gates: perhaps an indication of the older pre-Eudocian wall having a gateway to Mount Sion west of the ancient Sion Gate (5), approximately on the spot of present *Bāb an-Nabī Dā'ūd.*

15 Diaconicon of the Basilica on Mount Sion (?) attached to the basilica in the south, for a time used as the Martyrium of St. Stephen. The identification is not beyond any doubt. Did this building correspond to the present Tomb of David on top of which is the traditional place of the Last Supper (*Coenaculum*)?

16 Church of the House of Caiphas, erected about 500, commemorating the contrition of St. Peter who disowned the Lord, and, of course, the place of the High Priest's Palace. This church was clearly located outside the pre-Eudocian wall of Jerusalem, about 60 m southwest of *Bāb an-Nabī Dā'ūd*. It is represented in reverse, like nrs. 7 and 8. The main entrance is south of the end of the secondary street leading from the *Decumanus*. This is probably an indication that the whole church was situated outside the older wall.

The next two churches, situated near the street *al-Wād* in the so-called Tyropoion Valley (see above p. 89), are controversial. The discussion with all arguments and counter-arguments cannot be presented here. The author of this booklet will confine himself to his own opinion, fully aware that it is not the last word in the debate.

17 Church of St. Sophia (?), supposed in Byzantine times to stand on the ruins of Pilate's Praetorium (Mark 15:16 and parallels; John 18:28). The site is first mentioned by the pilgrim of Bordeaux (*Itinerarium Burdigalense* 16f.) as being 'below', i.e. in the Tyropoion Valley. The church was built around 450 at the latest, according to Peter the Iberian (Raabe, p. 94), and destroyed by the Persians in 614 like all other churches in Jerusalem. A detailed description was given by the Piacenza pilgrim (ch. 23). The historical place of Pilate's Praetorium was undoubtedly the citadel (19), but later on the tradition changed its place more than once up to the Middle Ages when it was fixed at the Antonia fortress north of the ancient temple area. What is meant on the Madaba map? Possibly the site of the present church of Notre Dame du Spasme between the Austrian Hospice and the monastery of the Catholic Armenians, at the 4th station of the *Via Dolorosa* (H. Donner, *ZDPV 81, 1965, p. 49-55*).

18 Church of St. Cosmas and St. Damianus (?), the so-called 'penniless' (*Anargyroi*), mentioned in the List of the Slain together with the Nea Theotokos (12) and St. Sophia (17) (Peeters, *Analecta Bollandiana* 38, 1920, nrs. 5-7). The church on the Madaba map, probably to be identified with it, was situated near the present *Maḥkama*, not far from *Ṭarīq Bāb as-Silsila*, between Wilson's Arch and the Wailing Wall. The two columns in the southern wall seem to be an indication of a Tetrapylon (see above p. 89).

Finally, some selected other buildings which are surely or probably identifiable.

19 Citadel (*al-Qalᶜa*), on the right side of the Jaffa Gate (6). The Citadel of Jerusalem had been improved by Herod the Great: details are described by Fl. Josephus, *Jewish War* V:4 (§§ 161-171). The Herodian Citadel was protected by three strong towers, named after members of Herod's family: Phasaël, Hippicus, and Mariamne. Two of them are represented on the Madaba map, the bigger one identical with what is still called the 'Tower of David'. The first connection of the Citadel with king David was made by the Piacenza pilgrim (ch. 21): 'Then we climbed the Tower of David where he recited the Psalter. It is enormous, and has cells

in each of the rooms. The tower itself is a hollow square building without a roof.' We may assume that the pilgrim meant the whole fortress of which the tower proper was part. According to Cyrill of Skythopolis (Life of St. Theodosius, Life of St. Sabas), monks of the Anastasis lived around the Tower of David after 550. Whether this kind of monastery is indicated - perhaps by the red roof of the House of Caiphas (16) also serving as roof of the building below - or not, remains uncertain.

20 Patriarchal Quarter (?). North of the Church of the Anastasis (7) three secular buildings are shown, probably indicating the Patriarchal Quarter of the city. The buildings might be identified as follows (from right to left): the palace of the Patriarchs, built by the empress Eudocia according to Nicephoros Callistos, *Eccl. Hist.* XXV:50 (PG 146,1240); a Clergy House belonging to the Patriarchal Palace; the Patriarchal Hospice, mentioned in the *List of the Slain* (Peeters, *Analecta Bollandiana* 38, 1920, nr. 19).

21 Monastery of the *Spoudaei* (?), built under the Patriarch Elias of Jerusalem after 494 and situated near the Patriarchal Palace. According to Cyrill of Skythopolis, a church of the Mother of God was there.

22 Temple Esplanade (*Ḥaram aš-Šarīf*), indicated by a black line of cubes only. The ancient temple area was ruined and desolate in Byzantine times, and the Christians did not take very much interest in it. The religious traditions maintained there had mostly been transferred to the Church of the Anastasis.

23 Fortress of Antonia (?), more precisely an unidentified building on the ruins of the Antonia.

24 Public Baths of Jerusalem (?), standing approximately on the spot of modern *Ḥammām as-Sulṭān*. The baths (δημοσία) are mentioned in the *Chronicon Paschale* (PG 92,613).

25 Staircase in front of the southern wall of the Temple Area (?). What we see is a quadrangle within a black line, divided by three black lines into smaller quadrangles, each containing two rows of yellow-greyish cubes, the whole originally continuing southwards. We may have here the large staircase leading up to the southern wall of the ancient Temple Area which has been recently discovered and renewed. Other scholars considered it a representation of the Wailing Wall, a much less probable solution, especially because of the division into smaller sections.

APPENDIX: FRAGMENTS

On the left, i.e. north of the main part of the mosaic, two fragments are preserved: the first one (A) at the northern side of the central nave near the second pillar (counted from the east), the second one (B) near the northern wall of the present church, approximately in the latitude of fragment A. A third fragment (C) was found in a private house at Madaba and was interpreted by J. Germer-Durand and Ch. Clermont-Ganneau as belonging to the Madaba map.

Fragment A

The fragment shows a section of the Galilaean mountains, bordered in the west by a plain. At the right edge we see the fragmentary representation of a village with a red-roofed church, and above it the inscription

ΑΓΒΑΡΩ[Ν]
Agbaron.
This is most probably identical with *ᶜAkbara* (coord. 197-260), about 2.5 km south of *Ṣafad* in Upper Galilee, mentioned by Fl. Josephus, *Jewish War* II:20:6 (§ 573) under the name 'Ακχαβάρων πέτρα 'the rock of the Akchabarites'. If this identification is correct, the three circles beneath the representation might be the waters of Merom (Josh. 11:5.7) where Joshua slew the king of Hazor. The village north of Agbaron could be *Ṣafad* (coord. 196-263) itself, and the other one west of it, Merom (= present *Mērōn*, coord. 191-265). The plain seems to be the plateau west of *Ṣafad* (H. Donner, *ZDPV 83, 1967, p. 30-32*).

Fragment B

The fragment, about 1.25 m long and 0.50 m wide, was first published in 1895 by J. Germer-Durand. At that time, it contained a piece of the Mediterranean Sea with the representation of a ship. This part, however, is lost. In 1965 only mountain chains were visible, with valleys or plains in between. The situation of the fragment in the present church and its relation to the other preserved parts of the map make it improbable that it is the northernmost part of Upper Galilee. We are already north of River Leontes (*Nahr Līṭānī*) in southern Lebanon. The remains of two inscriptions are visible:

ΜΩ̣[Μω[

ΠΕ.[πε.[

Unrestored and unidentifiable.

2. Ζ[ΑΒΟΥΛΩΝ ΠΑΡΑΛΙΟϹ ΚΑΤΟΙ]ΚΗϹ̣[ΕΙ ΚΑΙ ΠΑΡΑΤΕΝΕΙ ΕΩϹ ϹΙΔΩΝΟϹ]

Ζαβουλων παράλιος κατοικήσει καὶ παρατενεῖ ἕως Σιδωνος
Zabulon (= Zebulun) will dwell by the seashore, and (his border) will extend towards Sidon

This is an excerpt from the benediction on Zebulun in Gen. 49:13 according to the Greek Septuagint version (similar to nrs. 28, 41, 65). Historically, the tribal area of Zebulun was in the western part of Lower Galilee. The interpreters, however, took the phrase 'towards Sidon' verbatim and assumed the extension of Zebulun into present Lebanon (H. Donner, *ZDPV 83, 1967, p. 32f.*).

Fragment C

This fragment was found in the corridor of a private house at Madaba. It was published by J. Germer-Durand in 1895 and interpreted by Ch. Clermont-Ganneau (*PEFQSt* 1901, p. 241) as belonging to the Madaba map. The inscription ran as follows:

ϹΑΡΕΦΘΑ [Η] ΜΑΚΡΑ ΚΩ[ΜΗ] ΟΠΟΥ ΤΕΚΝ[ΟΝ ΗΓΕΡΘΗ ΕΝ Τ]Η ΗΜΕΡΑ ΗΚΕΙΝΗ

Σαρεφθα ἡ μακρὰ κώμη ὅπου τέκνον ἠγέρθη ἐν τῇ ἡμέρᾳ ἠκείνῃ (erroneously for ἐκείνῃ)

Sarephtha the large village where the child was raised to life that day

I Kings 17:9f.17-24; Luke 4:26; *Eus.On.* 162:1f.; also mentioned by Christian pilgrims and Early Fathers. The village is identical with *Ṣarafand* in Lebanon. – This fragment, however, has totally disappeared. Considering the extension of the mosaic map to the north and its position in the present church, it seems highly improbable that the fragment ever belonged to the Madaba map. We have to draw the conclusion that mosaics similar to the map also existed elsewhere at Madaba.

Selected Bibliography

J. Germer-Durand, La carte mosaïque de Madaba (Paris 1897).

W. Kubitschek, Die Mosaikkarte Palästinas. Mitteilungen der Geographischen Gesellschaft Wien, 43 (1900) p. 335-380.

A. Schulten, Die Mosaikkarte von Madaba und ihr Verhältnis zu den ältesten Karten und Beschreibungen des heiligen Landes. Abhandlungen der Königl. Gesellschaft der Wissenschaften zu Göttingen, Philolog.-histor. Klasse, NF 4, Nr. 2 (Berlin 1900).

A. Jacoby, Das geographische Mosaik von Madaba. Die älteste Karte des heiligen Landes. Ein Beitrag zu ihrer Erklärung. Studien über christliche Denkmäler 3 (Leipzig 1905).

P. Palmer - H. Guthe, Die Mosaikkarte von Madeba. I. Tafeln (Leipzig 1906).

R.T. O'Callaghan, Madaba (Carte de). Dictionnaire de la Bible (ed. L. Pirot et A. Robert), Suppl. V, fasc. 26 (1953) p. 627-704.

M. Avi-Yonah, The Madaba Mosaic Map. With Introduction and Commentary (Jerusalem 1954).

H. Donner - H. Cüppers, Die Mosaikkarte von Madeba. Tafelband. Abhandlungen des Deutschen Palästina-Vereins (Wiesbaden 1977).

M.-J. Lagrange, La mosaïque géographique de Mâdaba. RB 6 (1897) p. 165-184.

E. Stevenson, Di un insigne pavimento in musaico esprimente la geografia dei luoghi santi scoperto in una basilica cristiana di Madaba nella Palestina. NBAC 3 (1897) p. 45-102.

Ch. Clermont-Ganneau, The Land of Promise, mapped in Mosaic at Madeba. PEFQSt 1901, p. 235-246.

H. Guthe, Das Stadtbild Jerusalems auf der Mosaikkarte von Madeba. ZDPV 28 (1905) p. 120-130.

F.-M. Abel, Le Sud Palestinien d'après la carte mosaïque de Madaba. JPOS 4 (1924) p. 107-117.

M. Gisler, Jerusalem auf der Mosaikkarte von Madaba. Das Heilige Land 56 (1912) p. 214-227.

V.R. Gold, The Mosaic Map of Madeba. BA 21 (1958) p. 50-71.

P. Thomsen, Das Stadtbild Jerusalems auf der Mosaikkarte von Madeba. ZDPV 52 (1929) p. 149-174.192-219.

H. Donner, ZDPV 79 (1963) p. 59-89.

H. Donner, ZDPV 81 (1965) p. 43-46.49-55.

H. Donner - H. Cüppers, Die Restauration und Konservierung der Mosaikkarte von Madeba. Vorbericht. ZDPV 83 (1967) 1-33. Taf. 1-12.
H. Donner, Mitteilungen zur Topographie des Ostjordanlandes anhand der Mosaikkarte von Madeba. ZDPV 98 (1982) p. 174-190.
H. Donner, Das Nildelta auf der Mosaikkarte von Madeba. Fontes atque Pontes, eine Festgabe für H. Brunner. Ägypten und Altes Testament 5 (1983) p. 75-89.
C. Andresen, Betrachtungen zur Madebakarte in Göttingen. Pietas, Festschrift für B. Kötting. Jahrbuch für Antike und Christentum, Ergänzungsband 8 (1980) p. 539-558.
P. Donceel-Voûte, La carte de Madaba: Cosmographie, anachronisme et propaganda. RB 95 (1988) p. 519-542.

List of Abbreviations

1. Biblical Books

Gen.	Genesis (1. Book of Moses)
Exod.	Exodus (2. Book of Moses)
Numb.	Numbers (4. Book of Moses)
Deut.	Deuteronomy (5. Book of Moses)
Josh.	Joshua (Book of)
Judg.	Judges (Book of)
I/II Sam.	I/II Samuel (Book of)
Is.	Isaiah (Book of)
Jerem.	Jeremiah (Book of)
Am.	Amos (Book of)
Ps.	Psalms
I/II Chron.	I/II Chronicles
I Macc.	I Maccabees (Book of the)
Matth.	Gospel of St. Matthew

2. Books and Periodicals

BA	The Biblical Archaeologist
CSEL	Corpus Scriptorum Ecclesiasticorum Latinorum
Eus.On.	Eusebius, Onomasticon of Biblical Place Names
GCS	Die griechischen christlichen Schriftsteller
JPOS	Journal of the Palestine Oriental Society
NBAC	Nuovo Bolletino di Archeologia Cristiana
PEFQSt	Palestine Exploration Fund, Quarterly Statements
PEQ	Palestine Exploration Quarterly
PG	Migne, Patrologia Graeca
Raabe	R. Raabe, Petrus der Iberer (1895)
RB	Revue Biblique
ZDPV	Zeitschrift des Deutschen Palästina-Vereins

3. Other Abbreviations

ch.	chapter(s)
ed.	edited by
e.g.	for example
etc.	and so on, and others
fasc.	fascicle
hist.	historiae (stories)
hist.eccl.	historia ecclesiastica (church history)
i.e.	that is
nat. hist.	naturalis historia (natural history)
NF	Neue Folge (new series)
p.	page(s)
pl.	plate(s)
f., ff.	following(s)
Suppl.	Supplement(s)